2⁰⁰

MW01141712

Presented To:

_____

From:

_____

Date:

_____

THE
NEW
NORMAL

EXPERIENCING THE
UNSTOPPABLE MOVE OF GOD

MARK A. WYATT

DESTINY IMAGE. PUBLISHERS, INC.
P.O. Box 310, Shippensburg, PA 17257-0310

"Promoting Inspired Lives."

This book and all other Destiny Image, Revival Press, MercyPlace, Fresh Bread, Destiny Image Fiction, and Treasure House books are available at Christian bookstores and distributors worldwide.

For a U.S. bookstore nearest you, call 1-800-722-6774.
For more information on foreign distributors, call 717-532-3040.
Reach us on the Internet: www.destinyimage.com.

ISBN 13 TP: 978-0-7684-4093-5
ISBN 13 Ebook: 978-0-7684-8874-6

For Worldwide Distribution, Printed in the U.S.A.

1 2 3 4 5 6 7 / 15 14 13 12 11

DEDICATION

This book is dedicated to my father, Gene A. Wyatt Sr., and in memory of my mother, Betty Wyatt. Their unwavering commitment to me and my walk with God set me on the path that I gladly walk today. And every step says, "Thank you."

ACKNOWLEDGMENTS

The care and feeding of me has been the unenviable task of many people over the years, including:

John Dodd—the pastor who baptized me at age seven and who, as a member of my church now, makes my task a joy and not a burden. John and his wonderful wife, Norma, are what I aspire to be when I grow up.

Dr. Fred H. Wolfe—the pastor under whom I grew, was discipled, called, and grounded in the Word and in the faith. Brother Fred, you continue to inspire and model what a true pastor is. Thank you for introducing me to so many giants and so much truth.

Bishop Levy Knox and Lady Delia—my 3 A.M. friends and covenant partners in the Kingdom. You have only just begun. It is the joy of my heart to *walk* with you!

Dr. Jack Taylor—I had received some of the Kingdom before you came along, but it was your hands that put the balm on my eyes so that I could actually see what was right in front of me. I am forever grateful for your commitment to the King and His Kingdom. Few men deserve the right to proclaim His rule like you. You've earned it.

Jim Hylton—If anyone had told me when I first heard you speak more than 30 years ago that someday we would be calling each other just to chat, I would not have imagined how I could find myself in your circle. And yet, here we are. You have welcomed me in as an equal (which I certainly am not) and as a friend (which I certainly am). Every time we speak, I am amazed that I actually have your number in my phone's contact list.

My fathers in the Fellowship of Connected Churches and Ministries: T.D. Hall, Dudley Hall, Doug White, Peter Parris, and Terry Moore. It would take a whole page to thank you for all you have deposited into me. But of all the things you have given me, the greatest of these is love. Thank you.

My brothers in the Fellowship of Connected Churches and Ministries and the Opportunity for Unity Ministry Network—you have all saved my life in so many ways. To quote Clarence Oddbody, Angel Second Class, when he inscribed his copy of *Tom Sawyer* for George Bailey, "Remember, George, no man is a failure who has friends."

The saints at Deeper Life Fellowship—you are living examples of how a church makes a pastor's job look easy. It is an honor to serve you. Long live the Deep Sheep!

My incredible staff—Neal and Pam Bataller, Annette Oden, and Justin Benoit. I am honored to call you my friends. You have wept, laughed, loved, and bled right along with me. This book is yours as much as mine.

My in-laws, Milton and Ann Varner. Thank you for being patient with that long-haired boy who came for your daughter. I could not have gotten this far without your help.

And saving the best for last, thank you to my beautiful, brilliant, gifted wife, Mary Ann, and the absolute greatest children a father could never deserve: Samuel, Sarah, Nathaniel, and Autumn. You, my very own family, make every day an occasion of undying gratitude to the Father. I love you more than I can ever say, but I'll say it anyway, "I love you."

ENDORSEMENTS

"Good measure, pressed down, shaken together and running over" with passion for the move of God, exhortation to receive it, and wisdom to navigate its currents—that sums up Mark Wyatt's important work on how revival and the Kingdom of God intersect for a dynamism the Church longs for and the world needs. Mark is a good friend whose heart is full of love for Christ and whose pen follows his heart. I found myself over and over nodding my head with a quiet "Amen" as I read this book, as my spirit said "yes" to all its truths.

Alan Wright, Senior Pastor
Reynolda Church (EPC), Winston-Salem, North Carolina
Author, *Lover of My Soul* and *Free Yourself, Be Yourself*
President, Sharing the Light Ministries

When it comes to Kingdom outreach effectiveness, Mark Wyatt is a unique breed. His life and example have changed my life. Let his words change yours as well.

Steve Sjogren
Author, *Conspiracy of Kindness*
ServantEvangelism.com

Dr. Mark Wyatt is a breath of fresh air in a stagnating world. In his first book, *The New Normal: Experiencing the Unstoppable Move of God,* Dr. Wyatt takes you on a journey of revival to the cutting edge of living in the Kingdom of God. He provides unique insights combining experience and Scripture with lightness of touch that is sure to inspire and enlighten. My covenant relationship with this remarkable man has been both enriching and expanding. He is a "3 A.M." friend who walks the talk. His life is an example and his book a must. I highly recommend it for all who desire to make the shift from revival to experiencing the unstoppable move of God in Kingdom demonstration.

Dr. Levy H. Knox
Visionary & Founding Bishop
Living Word Christian Center
Mobile, Alabama

Mark Wyatt grew up in an expectant church environment. He learned to anticipate God's gracious renewal in the lives of his people. He now has fuller understanding of what the dynamics of the Kingdom of God include. His work on this subject will help us not only expect God's revelation of himself, but to embrace it for our good.

Dudley Hall
Author, *Grace Works* and *Incense and Thunder*

This is a book containing fresh new insights into what God is saying to His family today. I heartily recommend that you take time to hear from the mouth of God as Mark has heard. You will hear what Mark heard, but you will also hear what you need to hear and in some cases even hear much more than Mark heard. His hearing heart was open to all God had for him. God has no less for you. Listen, learn, and know the things God has prepared for you—things that will usher you into a new way of thinking, living, believing, and enjoying God's presence.

Jim Hylton
Author, *The Supernatural Skyline: Where Heaven Touches Earth*

"*What should be a stepping stone can become a stumbling block. What should be a gateway can become a goal. What could be a thoroughfare can become a terminal.*"

Leonard Ravenhill, *Why Revival Tarries*

CONTENTS

FOREWORD

I write many forewords, introductions, endorsements, and the like, all of which I enjoy. No two reading experiences are the same. All the readings are good, some are excellent, a few are beyond excellence, and precious few are what I call "rare." The book you hold in your hand is rare, not old-rare, or weird-rare, but not-many-in-its-class rare. Any one of its chapters is worth the investment of time and cost.

There is no doubt that *The New Normal* deals with two of the most relevant components in history: the Kingdom of God and the phenomenon of revival. The first thing most readers will take note of is that this book is pertinent. It relates to, well, everything that we think about in our lives as we seek to relate to God, others, and ourselves. Statement after statement, like a hammer, shatters traditional thinking and begins to build thought patterns that reveal the obvious. Much of what we have been looking for seems to have been hidden in plain sight.

The next thing to be noticed is that it is progressive. You may get the notion early in the reading—at least I did—that here is a destination we are moving toward, not just a conclusion to be reached. Without being argumentative or condescending, Mark Wyatt quietly and convincingly joins the message of the Kingdom of God and the mystery of spiritual awakening into a single thought process. And you awaken to the fact that the two have always belonged together. With powerful illustrative material and a combination of tasteful humor and creative thinking, the author introduces us to both subjects—the Kingdom and revival—as one new issue for our consideration. And it's a fit!

Many messages are lost because of common mistakes in approaching the reading experience: a reading fatigue based on complexity (too many words) and paralyzing familiarity of the been-there-done-that presumption. There seems to be in this book an inherent prevention of these mistakes. The movement of the thought patterns is neither boring and overstated, nor fleeting and spoken lightly. Catchy phrases dot the landscape of this work, making the journey from origin to destination a delightfully un-boring time.

By the time the experience is over, you are apt to emerge with the feeling that a vital introduction to a new friend has been effected. I suppose it's sort of like knowing two individuals who have courted for a time and then one day are pronounced husband and wife and we are introduced to one new entity, "Mr. and Mrs. _____." And in this new combination, two people, the same individuals they have been all along, become a new expression of purpose and unity.

Thanks, Mark, for bringing two seemingly separate and vital subjects together and pronouncing them one! Powerful! You have given us the feeling that we've only begun. Each subject will prove to give new meaning to the other.

Jack Taylor
Dimensions Ministries

INTRODUCTION

August 1996

It was my second night. I had driven 700 miles and stood in the summer sun for 12 hours, two days in a row, just to be here. Thousands of people, just as hungry as I was, milled around me, excited chatter drifting here and there throughout the day. Some were coming every week from nearby cities; some had traveled much farther than I had. Like me, they had heard that revival was here.

The first night, I was moved by the worship and impressed with the integrity of the message, but I was amazed at the sight of hundreds of people running to the altar. Merchant Marines outran young professionals, keeping pace with teenagers and older people all hurrying to respond to the Spirit of God. The altar was flooded with all kinds of people, and I couldn't take my eyes off the big, burly, bearded man with the bandana on his head and a dirty black t-shirt. He was on his knees on the altar steps, his shoulders bouncing gently as he sobbed openly. While the music played, the evangelist paused in his appeal, walked to the big man, stood near him, and through tears of his own, said, "Sir, you came to give your heart to Jesus tonight, didn't you?"

"Yes, sir!" the big man choked out. "Yes, sir!"

I had been to crusades. I had been to conferences. I had been to retreats, camps, and tent meetings. But right then, I knew. This was revival.

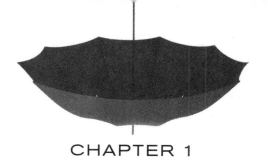

CHAPTER 1

BRING THE RAIN

As I write this, much of the United States is in the suffocating grip of a record-breaking heat wave. I just clicked over to a news website and was greeted by the headline: "Drought leaves 1.5 million hungry bats in Austin." The article goes on to explain that the world's largest urban bat colony there in Austin is starving because the drought has destroyed the crops that attract the bugs that attract the bats. In Kansas City, as many as 18 people have died from the heat, most of them young adults between the ages of 18 and 44. And in many other areas of the country, from Chicago to Baltimore, the oppressive heat and dry air are pandemic.

My wife and I grew up on the Alabama Gulf Coast, but after seminary, we lived in the North Dallas area for about 15 years, so I came to know about Texas summers. Our oldest son was born during one of those seemingly endless droughts of absolutely no rain, and temperatures over 100 degrees every single day for over 40 days. I remember some years, wishing someone would just hit me in the head and knock me out so that I could wake up in the fall. I was used to southern summer thunderstorms, the kind that would just pop up everywhere at about two o'clock in the afternoon, every afternoon. But in Texas, I could merely step out into the sunlight and feel myself start to bake, the air so hot that I could barely draw a breath. Depression would really begin to set in, though, when the weather forecaster would say that the 15-day outlook was exactly the same as the last 15 days. Unrelenting heat. Parched, cracked ground. Lakes and reservoirs dangerously low. With no end in sight.

But then, one day, out of nowhere, the sky would fill with clouds. They would billow up together, dark and gray, mingling across the sky like mourners in a funeral parlor. And then, finally, the rain would fall. And in the next few minutes, the streets would be filled with people coming out of their houses to stand in their yards, driveways, and cul-de-sacs, faces turned up, drinking in the rain. We gave no thought to getting wet, no thought to running for cover. This was what we had been waiting for, longing for, praying for. This was the water of life.

And so we wait for revival. We push through life, dry, thirsty, bowing under the oppressive weight of everyday existence, but we know there is more. We have tasted the rain before, we have stood in its life-giving flow, we have been refreshed by the waters of revival. We remember times when the love of God has overwhelmed our hearts. We can still point out the place where we stood when the mercy of God broke our pride and we wept with humility and joy as the Father washed us clean. And in the grip of the drought in our souls, we cry out for God to do it again: "Revive us again, fill each heart with thy love; may each soul be rekindled with fire from above!"

But we don't know how to get it. "What do we have to do to make God move?" we wonder. We hold conferences, we have prayer meetings; we get pastors in the city together to lead us in confessing our sins and assailing the heavens of brass. And still, it seems, nothing.

THE ROAD TO REVIVAL

"Daddy, where does revival come from?"

I have to admit that none of my children have asked me that question the way they have asked where *other* things come from. Still, it's a question I find myself asking the Father. Where does revival come from? Is it dependent on us, or is it a catch-as-catch-can "move of God"?

Jonathan Edwards, the preacher most associated with the First Great Awakening, believed that revival was an unpredictable, sovereign event, sent by God at the time of His choosing, and our responsibility was to respond rightly to it when it came. Charles Finney, who ministered during the Second Awakening, believed that we had some say in when and where revival came, and that if we would pray hard enough and "*break up your untilled ground*" (Hos. 10:12), God would, predictably, send revival when we were made ready enough.

My experience in the church was always a little of both—pray for revival really hard, but you never know when, or if, God will send it. It's like praying for rain and watching for lightning. It might come because you asked, but you really don't have a say in how it happens. Still, we would open our hymnals, and with passion and desperation, we would sing, "Lord, send a revival, and let it begin with me." And rightly so, because in every revival movement, it has seemed evident that prayer was the key. But what kind of prayer? Is revival "prayed down," or are we prayed "into position" for it? Does revival tarry, or are we to tarry for it?

Although the definition of revival is still debated, sometimes hotly, everyone seems to want it, at least their understanding of it. The purpose of this book is not to define revival or to justify or vilify any manifestation of it, but rather to lay out a scriptural approach to actually experiencing it. Revival can and should be experienced by every believer and every local church, and it isn't nearly as ethereal or mysterious as we have made it out to be. Revival is not a mysterious event to be prayed down, but the beginning of a level of life in the Kingdom of God in which we are to walk. In fact, I believe it is God's plan that all of us walk continually in an atmosphere of revival—all the time, every day. Now, with our preconceptions about what revival is, that would be impossible to do. It would involve manufacturing emotions, manifestations, or protracted meetings. I happen to enjoy all those things, but they are not in and of themselves revival, though they can be a result of revival. The reason we can all experience and live in revival is because revival is simply the experienced reality of the presence of the Kingdom of God. The purpose of this book is to help you understand what that means and how you can walk in it.

"IN WITH THE GOOD AIR…"

I know that I just said that the purpose of this book is not to define revival, but it would serve us well to think about it for just a moment. Think about it in natural terms: A man goes swimming at the beach, is pulled into deeper water by the undertow, and begins to struggle. Red-suited lifeguards run to the water's edge, dive in, and successfully make their way to the sinking man and bring him to shore to find that he has stopped breathing. His life is quickly ebbing away. However, with heroic effort, a lifeguard administers CPR, the water-logged man spews water, gasps, and begins to breathe again. What just happened? He has been revived!

Now what? Does he stay on the beach? Does he hold special meetings on that spot of sand to encourage others to have the same experience he had? Maybe for a little while. In fact, it would be understandable and appropriate for him to use that place, that event, as a springboard to honor the one who revived him, and encourage people to get to know the lifeguard, too. But he wouldn't build a house there. He wouldn't stay there forever. He would know that the reason he was revived was to continue to live his life, but hopefully, at a higher level of passion, understanding, and eternal perspective than he had before.

Revival appears to us as a wonderful, special, sovereign outpouring of God in a particular time and place. But, no matter how long the reviving lasts, it is still intended to culminate in years of living *after* the reviving. The act of being revived does not go on forever. At some point, life must take hold and sustain itself; otherwise, there has been no revival. Revival is an undeniable manifestation of the power and presence of God among us; but it is, by its very nature, the tip of the proverbial iceberg. *Revival is God bringing us back to life, so that we may go on beyond revival to live the life for which we were born in the first place.*

This is why we long for revival. Not just for the moment of it, not just for the feeling of it, but our hearts cry out to God, *"Will You not revive us again so that Your people may rejoice in You?"* (Ps. 85:6). We rejoice because we are alive again, and there is life to be lived. We need revival to bring us back, to shock us, to massage our hearts, to breathe new air into our spiritual lungs. We need it. But how do we get it?

"ARE WE THERE YET?"

The very first thing I want to do is ask the question that many of us have asked silently, but few have dared to put into audible speech: "How long do we really have to pray before we see revival?" I know, it's irreverent to even think such a thing, right? I mean, since we are supposed to be praying without ceasing anyway. If we are already thinking in terms of fulfilling a requirement, we have already missed the whole spirit of revival. I know. But still, the question nags at us.

We really want to see God do things in us, our churches, and our cities, that can only be explained by the fact that He is present and moving supernaturally in our midst. We want to see people being inexplicably drawn to our meetings, wandering in and saying, "How can I be saved?" We want to see wayward children, hard-hearted skeptics, and sin-blinded husbands break under the presence and anointing of the Holy Spirit, weeping and repenting. We want to hear the testimonies, sing the songs, be crushed in the bear hug of a biker ex-convict who just met Jesus. And it is good and right to want to see all those things. The desire to witness that kind of move of God is in you because it's part of your New Covenant package. People who don't know Jesus aren't really interested in any of that happening.

I remember being an older teenager and reading *The Invasion of Wales by the Spirit Through Evan Roberts* and thrilling to the stories of jailhouses shut down, churches starting in empty bars, and policemen forming barbershop gospel quartets because the crime rate was down and they had nothing else to do. At 15, I was overwhelmed by the need for revival as I sat and listened to the unction-filled challenges of Leonard Ravenhill, the fiery Scottish revivalist and author, for three days at a campground in Lindale, Texas, then praying with my friends until four or five o'clock in the morning, pleading for God to visit us in power. As a college student, I read Charles Finney's *Revival Lectures* and wept on every page, both in repentance and expectation. I sat on a worn-out couch in the Baptist Student Union and talked with Lewis Drummond, begging for morsels from him in the wake of his latest book, *The Awakening That Must Come.*

There were very special times at church as I grew up, times when the Holy Spirit would surprise us with conviction, repentance, reconciliation, a new hunger for holiness. Those times would come during a youth meeting, or in an impromptu prayer meeting, or on Sunday morning, when we could not let out the service. The people waiting for the second service would crowd in the doors, hungering, thirsting for a taste of what was happening. And I waited with tender heart and expectant spirit for the day when those things would happen in the church I would pastor, when God would let me be part of something so sweet, so powerful, so life-changing.

In July 1996, a group of friends from my home church in Mobile, Alabama, traveled to my small Baptist church in the Dallas-Fort Worth, Texas, area to help us with Vacation Bible School and hold special services at night. While they were there, I watched a long-time friend of mine. He was different. He was simply more in love with Jesus than I had ever seen. I asked him what was different, and he said, "Well, I don't know if you've heard about it, but there is a revival going on in Pensacola. I've been going there almost every night, and God has changed my life." The evangelist who had come with the team was part of this conversation, and he responded, "You've been going over there, too? You know, I have ten children, and I have been taking all of them over there one at a time, so that they can say they have actually seen a genuine, sustained move of God at least once in their lives."

They went on to describe the scene at Brownsville Assembly of God, how people would get in line at 3:15 A.M. just to make sure they would get into the building when it opened at 6 P.M., almost 15 hours later. Standing out in the Florida summer sun, people would wait for 12 hours or more just to go to church. Now, that I had to see. It is the fantasy of every pastor to have people line up early just to get a seat in church; and I was no different. Even if it wasn't my church, I had to at least know it was possible.

On the second night, in the overflow auditorium, I stood and sang the songs I was just learning as those of us who couldn't get into the main building watched the service on the big screen. And in that moment, on that spot of ground, standing between my wife and a few close friends, I felt as if my heart was about to burst. A sense of the presence of God like I had never had before welled up inside me, and it was all I could do to keep from breaking down into a crying mess. I was being overwhelmed. I knew that if I let go, there were going to be embarrassing, loud, uncontrollable sobs.

And in that same moment, I sensed the voice of God offering me a choice.

Just the previous Sunday, I had preached on how David danced before the Lord, and when his wife, Michal, despised him for it, she was cursed with barrenness for the rest of her life. I was in my third year of my first pastorate, and I already felt dry, frustrated, and barren. I didn't want to continue in that. And as I held back the tears, the Holy Spirit spoke to me, quietly, but firmly. "I asked David to dance for Me," He said. "Will you weep for Me?"

Time stood still. Everything else faded away except the song we were singing, the song that was coming from my mouth: "One thing I ask, one thing I seek: that I may dwell in your house, O Lord all of my days, all of my life, that I may see you, Lord."

And right then, I made a choice that changed my life. I knew that if I refused Him, He may not ask again. "Yes," I whispered in my heart. "I will weep for You." And the dam burst. Loud, racking, embarrassing weeping. And I didn't care in the least. And for the next 18 months, I couldn't get through a single sermon without weeping. And the hunger just kept growing.

HOW DO WE GET THERE FROM HERE?

The yearning, the hunger for revival is a good thing—and God is in it. So how do we get there? How do we get to be one of those who experience "the outpouring"? What is the secret?

As mentioned previously, in every historical account of revival, there is an undeniable element of prayer. So that must be it, right? Well, there are some who will say that *prayer* is the active ingredient, and that without it, revival is unattainable. Others, because of their research or experience, will say that *repentance* is the key. Still others, *reconciled relationships.* Others, *worship.* The fact is, determining what is the key factor in bringing a move of God to any particular group of people is impossible. It would be easier to identify a drop of water in the middle of an ocean and predict exactly when and where it will touch the shore.

Revival is, and should be, as dynamic and incalculable as God Himself. And yet, Hosea tells us that His coming is *"as sure as the dawn"* (Hos. 6:3). So we continue to look for the magic bullet. We read, we pray, we talk to people who have been part of revivals, and we seek that one special something that will turn the tide, the one thing that will *make* God come down to us.

Herein is the good news and the bad news. The *bad* news is that there is not, nor has there ever been, nor will there ever be, one mystery ingredient to revival. The *good* news is also that there is not, nor has there ever been, nor will there ever be, one mystery ingredient to revival. God is not hiding from us. He is not playing some sort of cosmic Clue game where we have to figure out who He will use, in what city, and what instrument He will employ. Revival really is not meant to be as mysterious or ethereal as we have made it to be. *Revival is, at its core, a continual awareness of the reality and manifestation of the Kingdom of God*. All of the outpourings we have ever seen, the times of refreshing, the awakenings—they have all been times when, for a brief moment, people lived in an awareness that God was all around them, and that He was speaking, calling, loving them, forgiving them, healing them. He was moving among them, and they knew it.

When revival stopped was when they lost that sense of the immediacy, that right-here-right-now reality of the Kingdom of God. That is why Jesus said to seek one thing before anything else. He said to seek the Kingdom (see Matt. 6:33). Could it be that He knew that when we find the Kingdom it changes everything? What if Jesus knew that when we live in a continual awareness of the manifest, present, and available Kingdom of God that we would be living in that state that we are always seeking? What if God's plan is for all of us to live in revival all the time? Is it possible? Can it really be done?

A NEW LEVEL OF LIVING

Randy Clark, modern-day revivalist, has said that when God sends a revival, the purpose of it is to introduce a new level of living so that the rest of the Body of Christ is called to rise up to that level and live there. Leonard Ravenhill said, in *Why Revival Tarries*: "We are so subnormal these days that normal New Testament experience seems abnormal."[1]

So let's ask the question: what if, every time in history that God has sent a revival, He intended His people to remain living at that level of intense awareness of Him, that level of holiness, passion, joy, boldness, healing, and hearing His voice? What would the Church look like today?

Now, I know that if you have ever been there when an outpouring comes down, the thought of living in that for the rest of your life can be draining. "There is no way," you might say. "I couldn't take it for long, even physically. I would burn up and disintegrate under that kind of intensity." I understand.

But I think there are two reasons why even the thought of it is so taxing: One is that it just isn't normal living for us. It is too far outside of our daily parameters of living. And two, it usually involves protracted meetings, which none of us can sustain forever. Revival, to us, is disrupting, even by definition. It is new life, when we had grown quite comfortable with our normal life, which, again by definition, is really non-life. It may not be exactly death, but it isn't exactly living either, not by God's standards. It's kind of like living in a spiritual coma. As far as the reality of the presence and power of the Kingdom of God goes, we aren't technically dead, but we have no quality of life. But instead of pulling the plug on ourselves, we keep hoping that maybe, someday, if we breathe just right, if we have the right dreams, maybe—just maybe—there will be an awakening. Maybe, just maybe, if we are good and diligent enough in our coma, God will have mercy on us and allow us to wake up and enjoy His presence.

HAVE I GOT GOOD NEWS FOR YOU!

If that tugs at your heart at all, if it sounds like where you are or where you have been, have I got good news for you. You don't have to hope against hope anymore. God has given us a promise about revival, about coming to us, about living in His presence. The really great part, though, is that He has already fulfilled His promise. In other words, everything you have been waiting for has already been provided—especially revival. And it's just for you. Turn to Hosea chapter 6 and let's see it.

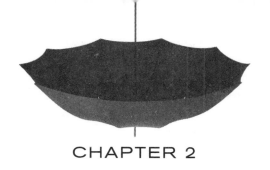

CHAPTER 2

"PLACES, EVERYONE!"

CULTIVATING A SPIRIT
OF EXPECTANCY

Come, let us return to the Lord. For He has torn [us], and He will heal us; He has wounded [us], and He will bind up our wounds. He will revive us after two days, and on the third day He will raise us up so we can live in His presence. Let us strive to know the Lord. His appearance is as sure as the dawn. He will come to us like the rain, like the spring showers that water the land (Hosea 6:1-3).

I have always loved and been drawn to this passage from Hosea 6. It always stirs me with anticipation; it fuels my longing for revival. At the same time, I had always been a little confused by this passage. If this really is a promise of revival, which I believe it is, what am I to make of the references to time? How long do I have to pray for revival? Hosea seems to say that it's only two days, maybe three. I can do that. But my experience tells me differently. I'm told we must pray for years, early in the morning, every morning, before God will consider that we have earned some sort of move. So what about the three days, then? Maybe it isn't a literal day. Maybe it's one of those "day as a thousand years" kind of days that I have heard so much about. If Hosea 6:1-3 isn't a promise that we will have revival after two days of praying, what is it? I'll give you a hint, and then I'll explain more later: Hosea 6:1-3 *is* a promise of revival, but it is a promise fulfilled, and the fulfillment of it is everything that you could hope for and more.

"COME, LET US RETURN..."

As we look at this passage of Scripture and see the promise of revival, we need to remember to ask ourselves something vitally important that applies any time we see Old Testament prophecy: How does this prophecy go all the way through Jesus? We are beginning to understand more and more in the Body of Christ that the Old Testament is not a stand-alone book that can be interpreted outside of Jesus. In his excellent book *A Passion for God's Story*, author Philip Greenslade illustrates this in the context of the genealogy of Jesus in Matthew chapter 1. Greenslade states:

> By saying that Jesus "fulfills" the Scriptures, Matthew does not mean that isolated predictive proof-texts

launched from the Old Testament land on-target in Jesus. Something much bigger than this is going on. Rather, Matthew seeks to show that the whole pattern of Israel's story is being gathered up and reproduced in Jesus. The entire story is being "filled-full" by Jesus. He embodies the vocation and destiny of his people. The "man who fits no formula" conforms his life to this scriptural shape.[2]

So let's take this passage from Hosea and run it all the way through the life, ministry, death, and resurrection of Jesus, and see where it comes out.

First, Hosea's plea to "*Come, let us return to the LORD,*" sounds suspiciously like the first word of Jesus' first sermon, "*Repent*" (Matt. 4:17). Charles Finney defined revival as "nothing else than a new beginning of obedience to God. Just as in the case of a converted sinner," says Finney, "the first step is a deep repentance, a breaking down of heart, a getting down into the dust before God, with deep humility, and a forsaking of sin."[3] It should come as no surprise to us that a prerequisite for being revived is repentance. How could we expect God to pour out His Spirit into an "unclean vessel"? In fact, most revival praying has started well at this point. We usually don't have a problem forsaking our sin, at least the best we know how, when we are praying for revival. We are not so presumptuous as to expect Holy God to wink at our sin and open the heavens.

But, if we really look at what Jesus was saying, it includes much more than being sorry for sin. When Jesus said, "*Repent,*"

He wasn't saying, "Feel sufficiently sorry for being bad." He was saying, "Change the way you have been thinking." This is made clear by the next phrase in His sermon, "*because the kingdom of heaven has come near!*" (Matt. 4:17). In other words, "I have arrived, and I brought My world with Me. There is a new Kingdom right here in front of you, and if you want to get in on it, you are going to have to learn to think differently from how you have thought before."

This, then, is the echo of Hosea's call to "*Come, let us return to the LORD.*" It is an act of changing, of going a different way from where you are currently headed. This was obviously a cry for the people of Hosea's own time. They had left God and had committed adultery in their relationship with Him.

Then the LORD said to me, "Go again; show love to a woman who is loved by another man and is an adulteress, just as the LORD loves the Israelites though they turn to other gods and love raisin cakes" (Hosea 3:1).

This is obviously not a command to stop buying Little Debbie® Raisin Crème Cakes, though it probably wouldn't hurt me to interpret it as such. It is the assignment to Hosea to marry an adulteress, a prostitute, to illustrate to Israel how God still loved them even though they had gone away from Him. God's call to them through Hosea was to "*come*" and "*return*," because "*a spirit of promiscuity leads them astray*" (Hos. 4:12). In 6:3, Hosea urges them to "*strive to know the LORD,*" because in their unrepentant mode,

42

Their actions do not allow [them] to return to their God, for a spirit of promiscuity is among them, and they do not know the LORD (Hosea 5:4).

The key to Israel's ability to turn from their sin was to change the way they were thinking—thus the promise of revival in chapter 6. Hosea was trying to get them to see that if they would just return to the Lord, then living under His rule and reign would be the best thing that ever happened to them. In other words, "Repent, because the Kingdom of heaven has come near you!"

WHERE DID *THAT* COME FROM?

Next, Hosea goes on to say some things that, quite honestly, I have always read aloud with great passion so that no one else would know that I had no idea what I was talking about. *"For He has torn [us],"* he says, *"and He will heal us; He has wounded [us], and He will bind up our wounds"* (Hos. 6:1). The more I learn about God's willingness and ability to heal people today, the more confusing it is to see those words in black and white in Scripture: *"He has torn us,"* and *"He has wounded us."* Does God really do that? If so, why, and did He enjoy it? Was He that angry with us in our sin? These questions speak directly to our view of the Father.

In order to understand this verse, we need to have a right perspective on where our wounds come from. There are two eternal truths that help this all make sense.

First, sin always has been, and always will be, destructive. It wounds you. Sin never helps you. As E. Stanley Jones, 20th century theologian and missionary to India, explains in his classic, *The Unshakable Kingdom and the Unchanging Person*, sin is not natural to us because we have been made in the image and likeness of God, and that includes a spiritual affinity for His Kingdom. We have been designed to operate at peak performance as we operate in accordance with, not in opposition to, the laws and principles of the Kingdom of God. This even applies to people who don't know the Lord.

If we live our lives according to the laws and principles of God's rule and reign, if we do what He says works best, we benefit. The Scriptures tell us that in our business dealings, we should be honest instead of cheating. No matter who you are, if you run your business honestly, it is good for you; if you cheat people, it will hurt you. You will be wounded by that sin. In the Kingdom, we are to love people and act lovingly to them. No matter who you are, if you are nice to people and treat them well, your life will be better for it. If you are mean to people, it will cost you. You will be wounded, and, in the case of being mean or cheating people, quite possibly literally. The truth remains that, *"Unless someone is born of water and the Spirit, he cannot enter the kingdom of God"* (John 3:5), but if anyone lives according to the eternal ways of God, it will bless him, and if he flaunts the laws and principles of the Kingdom, he will be wounded.

Sin is a foreign object in our spiritual body, and if we let it in, it will hurt us. E. Stanley Jones goes on to say that sin is as natural to us as sand in the eye, or acid on the hand.

We do not deny that sin is in human nature. It is there, and deeply so; it has corrupted man, and deeply so. But we do deny that it is natural. If it were natural, why should it corrupt him? If it were natural, man should blossom and bloom and be fulfilled in sin. Is he? The opposite. A man goes to pieces under sin—inevitably.[4]

Have you ever seen someone and thought, "He looks like he has had a hard life?" How does someone look like that? Usually when we refer to someone that way, we are talking about a hard life in terms of the consequences of sin. Maybe he drank too hard or too long, or smoked too much, or lived too angrily, or became too bitter. Whatever it is, it shows up in his body. If sin were good for us, or even neutral, how could it wreak such havoc? The fact is that sin, by its very nature, is destructive— and we cannot reason it to be any other way.

So, in one sense, God hasn't torn or wounded us, but He has watched with a broken heart while sin has ravaged our lives. Remember, God never takes direct action against us because of sin! His wrath against sin was poured out once and for all on Jesus as He became sin for us and our sin was nailed to the cross. God isn't angry anymore, and He has never been angry at you!

There is a second truth that speaks to this issue of being wounded; sometimes it takes getting wounded in order to get healed. For example, I am 49 years old, and I still hate shots. I don't whimper very loudly anymore at the sight of the needle, but all things being equal, I would rather not be stabbed with a sharp object. Sometimes, though, I willingly submit to the wound so that I can be healed. If I need a shot, I would rather bear the brief pain and get on to my healing than to be sick. If someone needs stomach surgery, then a kind and skillful surgeon will take an incredibly sharp knife, a scalpel, and wound him. The surgeon will cut the person open without a second thought. What's more, that person on the table is going to pay him a lot of money to do it. Why? Because if God has not yet intervened supernaturally, it is the next step in the person's healing. He wounds us to heal us.

If God is doing surgery on your life right now, submit to the love that you know He has for you, and look forward to the healing.

In Luke chapter 4, Jesus stands in the synagogue, opens the Scriptures to Isaiah 61, and reads His job description:

The Spirit of the Lord is on Me, because He has anointed Me to preach good news to the poor. He has sent Me to proclaim freedom to the captives and recovery of sight to the blind, to set free the oppressed, to proclaim the year of the Lord's favor (Luke 4:18-19).

The full text of what He read that day, as recorded in Isaiah, goes into a little more detail:

The Spirit of the Lord GOD is on Me, because the LORD has anointed Me to bring good news to the poor. He has sent Me to heal the brokenhearted, to proclaim liberty to the captives, and freedom to the prisoners; to proclaim the year of the LORD's favor, and the day of our God's vengeance; to comfort all who mourn, to provide for those who mourn in Zion; to give them a crown of beauty instead of ashes, festive oil instead of mourning, and splendid clothes instead of despair. And they will be called righteous trees, planted by the LORD, to glorify Him (Isaiah 61:1-3).

Now, that sounds like a Healer! Hosea promised, by the Spirit of God, that if God's people would return to Him, if they would repent, then He would heal them. That is exactly what Jesus said He came to do. His rule and reign, as King, would be to bring to repentant people—those willing to change—healing for their wounds. So, there it is again: Change the way you are thinking, and you can get in on all that the Kingdom of God is—right here, right now.

"I HAVEN'T GOT TIME FOR THE PAIN"

When Carly Simon recorded "Haven't Got Time for the Pain" in 1974, it was a wonderful declaration of the power of moving on from hurt into healing. The irony of the title phrase in our context is that even when we don't have time or room for the pain that we have caused ourselves, God does. The great truth of Hosea 6:1-2 is that even though we have torn and wounded ourselves, it is God who takes responsibility for the consequences of our sin, and provides the healing for it as well. Sounds like the essence of the Gospel, doesn't it?

Let's consider for a moment what was going on in Israel and Judah. Collectively, as the people of God, the Hebrews were once again in the middle of a well-worn cycle in their history. Typically, it went something like this: God promises to bless them if they obey the Covenant, and warns of punishment if they abandon it. They agree. Then they proceed to follow other gods, committing adultery on their Covenant Partner. Punishment ensues, at which point they repent and cry out for deliverance. God has mercy on them, hears their cries, sends deliverance, and they rejoice in forgiveness; until the next generation. Then they start the same cycle all over again.

Hosea's message comes in the middle of one of those cycles, so we can see that the wounds of Israel in Hosea's time are self-inflicted. In other words, God didn't actually tear them—they have torn themselves and are suffering the consequences of sin. God did not wound them—they have wounded themselves. And still, the Father takes responsibility for the place in which they find themselves.

Another place in Scripture where this truth is displayed is in the Book of Job. Look at this passage in Job 42:10-11:

And the LORD turned the captivity of Job, when he prayed for his friends: also the LORD gave Job twice as much as he had before. Then came there unto him all his brethren, and all his sisters, and all they that had been of his acquaintance before, and did eat bread with him in his

> *house: and they bemoaned him, and comforted him over*
> *all the evil that the LORD had brought upon him...* (KJV).

What?! *"The evil that the LORD had brought upon him"*? Wait a minute! Isn't it abundantly clear from the beginning of the story who is actually responsible for Job's suffering? God never afflicted Job. Satan did. Some will say that God "passively" afflicted him since He allowed it, but it still remains that the sender of Job's troubles was satan. But here, we see it again— God, in His sovereignty and Fatherhood, takes responsibility for the pain of His children. Why? So He can heal them. He never says, "Well, now look what you've done. Good luck dealing with that! It's not My fault your life is so messed up. Come see Me again when you get it together." And the reason He never says anything remotely like that is love. Real love. The love of a Father who embraces His children in the midst of their suffering, pulls them close, and heals their wounds, no matter from where those wounds have come.

THE DIFFERENCE BETWEEN WOUNDS AND DISCIPLINE

One more thing before we move on to the whole "two days, three days" promise: Don't make the mistake of applying the concept of discipline to every bad or uncomfortable thing that comes your way. Too often, in trouble, we go directly to Hebrews 12; we do not pass go, and we *certainly* don't collect anything! There is an all too pervasive, sadly mistaken idea that God is a Father who is constantly disciplining His children.

In fact, we have been told to watch for it and enjoy it, because that's proof that you are His:

> For the Lord disciplines the one He loves, and punishes every son whom He receives.... But if you are without discipline—which all receive—then you are illegitimate children and not sons (Hebrews 12:6,8).

And so, if we sin, and it wounds us, we believe we are being spanked, and we say, "Thank You, Sir, may I have another?" Or, if tragedy befalls us, we say, like Job's friends, we must have done something to deserve this chastening, and we are glad because at least it proves we are His.

I have to tell you, when I want to prove to my children that they are mine, spanking, grounding, and berating them is not the first thing that comes to mind. My children don't yearn for me to punish them so that they can feel secure. Discipline is not God's chosen method of expressing His love for you! In fact, we even understand with our own children that discipline and correction is only necessary for a short time. Don't we all hope that our children will mature to the point that they don't need discipline anymore because they have learned to make good choices?

In our home, we have a standing rule: Discipline is only given for disrespect and willful disobedience. We don't spank or ground or berate for spilling milk or tripping over a ninja sword and breaking its plastic hilt. I have noticed a pattern, though. All four of my children were disciplined more when they were younger. As they have matured, the discipline has become far more rare; and when it *is* necessary, the nature of it has changed. For Samuel, at 2 years of age, he might have had to sit in time out. At 13, we might have a serious talk in his room. At 17, he loses his cell phone. For Sarah, our 15-year-old, if a look of disappointment crosses my face, she will burst into tears and repent with much wailing. I don't have to do anything. Her conscience provides the discipline. The point is that all my children are wired differently, and they respond to different stimuli.

The root word of "discipline" is "disciple." God is not sitting in Heaven constantly doling out sentences to punish His children, whom He loves! If you want to see how Jesus described the Father, read Luke 15 again and put yourself in the shoes of the lost son. And, if you have been a Christian for a number of years and you think God is still disciplining you, I think I can help: Grow up, live like a son who loves the Father, and He'll stop.

Now, let's continue to take this passage from Hosea 6 all the way through Jesus, and see if it doesn't help us understand what the "days" really mean.

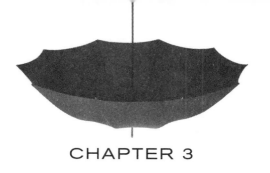

CHAPTER 3

HOW LONG, O LORD?

It would be one of the most grandiose understatements in the history of human language to say that John Hyde was a praying man. Born the son of a pastor in Carthage, Illinois, in 1865, Hyde became known as the Apostle of Prayer, or simply, Praying Hyde. His friend and biographer, Francis McGaw, wrote of him:

> The place where John Hyde met God was holy ground. The scenes of his life are too sacred for common eyes. I shrink from placing them before the public. But near the prayer closet of John Hyde we are permitted to hear the sighing and the groaning, and to see the tears coursing down his dear face, to see his frame weakened by foodless days and sleepless nights, shaken with sobs as he pleads, "O God, give me souls or I die!"

The following account is given of the end of his life, in 1811, one year before he died, as a friend convinced him to see a doctor in Calcutta, where Hyde was holding meetings:

> The next morning the doctor said: "The heart is in an awful condition. I have never come across such a bad case as this. It has been shifted out of its natural position on the left side to a place over on the right side. Through stress and strain it is in such a bad condition that it will require months and months of strictly quiet life to bring it back again to anything like its normal state. What have you been doing with yourself?" Dear Hyde said nothing, he only smiled. But we, who knew him knew the cause: his life of incessant prayer day and night, praying exceedingly with many tears for his converts, for his fellow-laborers, for his friends, and for the church in India!

And here is a description of revival in the context of John Hyde's ministry:

> At one time John Hyde was told to do something and he went and obeyed, but returned to the prayer room weeping, confessing that he had obeyed God unwillingly. "Pray for me, brethren, that I may do this joyfully."

> We soon learned after he went out that he had been led to obey triumphantly. He re-entered the hall with great joy, and as he came before the people, after having obeyed God, he spoke three words in Urdu and three

in English, repeating them three times, "Ai Asmani Bak," "O Heavenly Father."

What followed who can describe? It was as if a great ocean came sweeping into that assembly. Hearts were bowed before that Divine Presence as the trees of the wood before a mighty tempest. It was the ocean of God's love being outpoured through one man's obedience. Hearts were broken before it. There were confessions of sins, with tears that were soon changed to joy, and then to shouts of rejoicing. Truly, we were filled with new wine, the new wine of Heaven![5]

Few things can convince me that I'm not good enough for God like praying for revival. I pray, I repent, I worship, I weep. And nothing. Sure, I experience a degree of personal revival, but then again, how can you pray, repent, worship, and weep before God without getting some benefit from it? And as much as I enjoy a renewed and rekindled fellowship with the Father, still, what I am asking for is a move of God that would impact and affect everyone around me.

Especially as a pastor, when I pray for revival, what I hope for is that even before I open my mouth next Sunday, that when the people see my tear-filled eyes, that the Holy Spirit will fall upon them, brokenness will sweep through the room, and we will stay on our faces until people from all over the city, hearing about what is going on, clamor into our building and fall beside us. I am asking for something like John Hyde's experience.

And still, nothing.

So, obviously, I am the weak link. And, frankly, reading about "Praying Hyde" doesn't really help, it just reinforces the idea that if his commitment to prayer is what it takes to see revival, I will never see it, so I might as well stop asking.

So I stop.

But then I realize that God doesn't grade on performance, and because of grace I have as much chance as anybody at being part of that kind of outpouring. So I start praying again. And there I go 'round the revival bush, getting dizzier and wearier with every revolution.

Sound familiar?

And yet Hosea's promise, no...God's promise, hovers in front of me like an oasis that I have to believe is not a mirage, "*He will revive us after two days, and on the third day He will raise us up so we can live in His presence*" (Hos. 6:2).

A PROMISE FULFILLED

Second Corinthians 1:20 tells us that, "*Whatever God has promised gets stamped with the Yes of Jesus. In Him, this is what we preach and pray, the great Amen, God's Yes and our Yes together, gloriously evident...*" (MSG). If that is true, then it has to include Hosea 6, because that, as much as anything else in Scripture, is a promise of God. So, if it is already a yes in Jesus, what does that mean for us on this side of the cross? How do we preach and pray the yes of Jesus in context of this passage?

It really only takes a little different perspective to see it. Here is the question: What do the phrases "after two days revived" and "third day raised up" have to do with Jesus? You probably saw it before you even finished reading the question. Hosea was speaking to his own people about God's promise to restore fellowship with them; and at the same time, he was speaking prophetically about the coming Messiah. Let's break it down just a bit:

"He will revive us after two days..." (Hos. 6:2a). So there is some sort of revival, or life again, *after* the second day. "... *And on the third day He will raise us up*" (Hos. 6:2b). Now who does that sound like? When Jesus was revived in the tomb after two days dead, and raised up to a new resurrected life on the third day, He was fulfilling the promise given hundreds of years before that God would bring new life to His people, and they could now live in His presence!

Hosea 6:1-3 is not merely a prescription for how to lead a prayer meeting for revival. It is a declaration that 2,000 years ago God provided, through the ministry, death, and resurrection of His Son, the ability to live in a constant reality of revival glory.

So, here's the progression: We return to the Lord (repent), because Jesus said that He had come to make us whole again just like God promised in Hosea. Then, as we change our way of thinking and begin to comprehend that the Kingdom of

God is here right now, we see that Jesus was revived so that we could experience constant revival as the normal way to live. And living is what this is all about, *"...so we can live in His presence"* (Hos. 6:3c).

LIVING WELL

The Hebrew verb for "live" that is used here is *chayah*. It means "to be alive, to live, to keep alive."[6] It is used in the sense of flourishing, or to convey that an object is safe. When we speak about someone being alive, we might mean that his brain and heart are still working. When we speak of someone living, we usually mean a little more than that, but not much. Living may include eating, drinking, talking, working, mowing the lawn, buying groceries. Someone in a coma may be alive, but we don't call that living.

At this point, though, we settle for far too little. To us, living is nothing more than a reasonable amount of activity in a continuation of years. We even think of our jobs as a primary tool of extending our existence—we "make a living."

God, on the other hand, has a different idea of what it means to be alive. Hosea says that on the third day we were raised up to live—to *chayah,* to flourish in safety—in His presence. For our Father, living is much more than our ability to take another breath. It is the freedom to breathe. It is more than our heart pumping blood. It is our heart beating in rhythm to the cadence of the Holy Spirit.

This is the same Hebrew word used in Ezekiel 37 when the prophet was instructed to call to the winds and command them to blow on the newly fleshed bodies in the valley:

> *He said to me, "Prophesy to the breath, prophesy, son of man. Say to it: This is what the Lord GOD says: Breath, come from the four winds and breathe into these slain so that they may live!" So I prophesied as He commanded me; the breath entered them, and they came to life and stood on their feet, a vast army* (Ezekiel 37:9-10).

One moment the valley floor was littered with corpses. The next moment, it was filled with a vast army. One thing made the difference: They were revived. We can actually use the *re-* in revival accurately here, because the fact that they started as bones means that they were once alive, but now were dead. So revival came, and they were raised up to live in His presence, a vast army.

TIMES OF REFRESHING

When Hosea uses the word "presence" (or "sight" in KJV), it is the Hebrew masculine plural (isn't that interesting?) noun meaning "face."[7] Often, in Hebrew culture, the face could be a substitute for the whole person. So when God says that we are to seek His face, He is not talking about His face as opposed to any other part of Him. He is saying that we are to seek His presence. This is echoed in Acts 3:19: *"Therefore repent and turn back, that your sins may be wiped out so that seasons of refreshing may come from the presence of the Lord."* The Greek word for "presence" here is *prosopon*, which means "countenance,"[8] or, once again, face. The word for "refreshing" is *anapsuxis*, meaning "a recovery of breath."[9] That sounds like the Ezekiel incident again, doesn't it? So in Acts, we could say that Peter is talking about revival—new breath.

In Acts 3:19, the word that is translated "come" in the sentence: "...*so that seasons of refreshing may come from the presence of the Lord*," is from the root word *eltho*, which means "accompany, appear, bring, fall out, grow; which do not otherwise occur."[10] Did you get that? These are things that do not otherwise occur! In other words, seasons of refreshing can *only* come from the presence of God. Do you need refreshing? Do you need a recovery of breath? Do you need revival? There is only one place to go. But how can you *go* to the presence of God when He is already here?

HAS GOD EVER BEEN ABSENT?

Do you remember in school when the teacher called the roll? How were you supposed to answer? "Present!" Of course, you always had that one kid who thought it was funny to say "President!" every day. Really not that funny after the first week. And, to be fair, those of us who grew up in the Deep South were allowed to holler, "Here!" Regardless, whether we were proper enough to say "Present" or casual enough to say "Here," what were we saying? "I am in the room, and I am revealing myself to you by speaking. Why? Because you are too lazy to just look for me." I know, teachers aren't really lazy, and I'm not picking on them here, but the fact is that this is how we treat God. He's already here, and if we just look for Him, we might not be so uptight about whether or not we are hearing Him all the time. So, before we answer the roll call, we are already present in the room; but when called upon, we are required to reveal our presence.

Now we come to the difference between the omnipresence of God and the manifest presence of God. Often, when we start talking about revival, we speak of "getting into the presence of God," and frankly, that concept is both right and wrong. It is wrong in the sense that God is already present. He is omnipresent, everywhere at the same time. I read a popular saying today: "God could not be everywhere at once so He invented mothers." That's a nice sentiment for mothers, but what an affront to Almighty God! Of course He can be everywhere at once.

So how can you "get into" God's presence when you can never be out of God's presence? The answer: What we call "getting into" God's presence is when the omnipresence of God becomes revealed to us, when the invisible world invades the world of our senses, and we begin to actually *experience* the God who is present.

THE KINGDOM OF GOD IS LIKE...STAR TREK

One of my favorite "Star Trek" (the original series) episodes illustrates this nicely. Captain's log. Stardate 5710.5.

The Starship Enterprise receives a distress call from the planet Scalos. The small group of Scalosians claim to be the last survivors of a population of 900,000. However, when the Enterprise reaches Scalos, they find an apparently deserted city. Upon returning to the Enterprise, though, strange goings-on become evidence that aliens have beamed aboard with them. Eventually, they discover that something in the Scalosian water makes anyone who drinks it become hyper-accelerated. So, the hyper-accelerated people are right there beside everyone, but the people in normal-time mode can't see them because they are moving so fast. Then, within an hour, everything is made right.

The point is that the invisible and the visible exist simultaneously, side by side, but only those whose senses have been attuned to the new reality can experience both. Jesus said that the Kingdom of God is like *"yeast that a woman took and mixed into 50 pounds of flour until it spread through all of it"* (Matt. 13:33). Once you mix yeast into a lump of dough, you can't see the yeast anymore. It becomes invisible, but it's still there, doing what it is supposed to do. It is changing the whole lump.

The Kingdom of God is here. It may be hidden, but it's working.

The same thing happens to Zechariah, John the Baptist's father, in Luke 1:

One day Zechariah was serving God in the Temple, for his order was on duty that week. As was the custom of the priests, he was chosen by lot to enter the sanctuary of the Lord and burn incense. While the incense was being burned, a great crowd stood outside, praying. While Zechariah was in the sanctuary, an angel of the Lord appeared to him, standing to the right of the incense altar (Luke 1:8-11 NLT).

The angel begins to tell Zechariah that he and Elizabeth will have a son, and what an incredible man of God that son will be. When Zechariah questions the veracity of this report, the angel answers with one of my favorite passages in the whole Bible:

Zechariah said to the angel, "How can I be sure this will happen? I'm an old man now, and my wife is also well along in years." Then the angel said, "I am Gabriel! I stand in the very presence of God. It was He who sent me to bring you this good news! But now, since you didn't believe what I said, you will be silent and unable to speak until the child is born. For my words will certainly be fulfilled at the proper time" (Luke 1:18-20 NLT).

Can't you see the look on Gabriel's face? "What do you mean, 'how can I know?' Who do you think you're talking to? I'm Gabriel! I mean, come on, I just stepped out from the presence of God, which, you may remember, is right on the other side of this veil. Sheesh!"

Zechariah was right up against the invisible, but he didn't see it until it was revealed to him, and even then, he wasn't so sure. This is one of the wonderful mysteries of the Kingdom. Kingdom reality cannot be discovered, it must be revealed. You can dig and sort and word study and memorize commentaries, but for any of us to really perceive the invisible Kingdom of God, God Himself has to reveal it. Our intellect can't take us there. What we are living in isn't reality, it's virtual reality. *"So we do not focus on what is seen, but on what is unseen; for what is seen is temporary, but what is unseen is eternal"* (2 Cor. 4:18). Kingdom reality must be made manifest to us. Merriam-Webster defines "manifest" as "readily perceived by the senses and especially by the sight."

THE MANIFEST PRESENCE OF GOD

This, then, is the manifest presence of God. It is the omnipresence of God revealed to us so that we can actually perceive it with our senses. The invisible world, or the most real world, presses upon the visible, the temporal world; and we sense it and react to it. Sometimes we fall on our face, sometimes we just fall. We may weep, we may laugh, or we may tremble or grow completely still. We confess, we repent, we speak with boldness, and we love our brothers and sisters. We talk about Jesus more easily, we pray more fervently, we sing with more passion. All of these things that we associate with revival are simply what happens when our reality collides with God's reality.

Hosea said that we were to live in His presence. But we treat the manifest presence of God as "a nice place to visit, but I wouldn't want to live there." Why not? Doesn't God want us to live there? If not, where else are we to live? Did Jesus die for us to live—to *really live*—any other way?

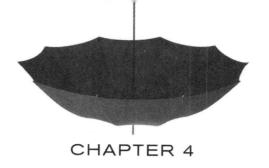

CHAPTER 4

WALKING IT OUT

Now we have to ask the next two obvious questions: What would it look like if we were to live in a constant awareness of the Kingdom of God? And, how do we walk it out? Paul gives us a wonderful answer, and he even uses the word "walk." One warning, though: The Scripture we will look at has been so mis-preached that you might balk at it, but stay with me for a few minutes, and I think you might see it in a brand-new way.

Apostle Paul gives us a simple handbook for Kingdom living in one verse: *"I say then, walk by the Spirit and you will not carry out the desire of the flesh"* (Gal. 5:16). When I was growing up, here's the way I read and understood this verse: "OK, you guys are really messing up, so stop it. Stop walking in the flesh, and walk in the Spirit." Every time I heard this passage preached, that was the gist of it. "Buckle down. Straighten up. Act right. Stop being bad and start being better."

The problem was that I didn't know how to do any of that. So I would repent for not being disciplined enough, I would recommit to a daily quiet time early in the morning, and I would vow to stop listening to secular music. And I called that walking in the Spirit. But that isn't at all what Paul is saying in Galatians 5:16. This verse is not a command, it's a promise. It isn't "Stop fulfilling the desires of your sinful nature, and start walking in the Spirit." Rather, *"What I am saying is this: run your lives by the Spirit. Then you will not do what your old nature wants"* (Complete Jewish Bible).[11] Now there's a promise!

THOSE FOOLISH GALATIANS

We tend to be a bit hard on the Christians in the church at Galatia because Paul is pretty exasperated; and even though he does call them "foolish," he really isn't upset at them. It is clear who has his ire up in verse 12: *"I just wish that those trouble-makers who want to mutilate you by circumcision would mutilate themselves"* (NLT). Try teaching *that* verse all by itself!

Paul is angry at the Judaizers, the group of Jews who were coming to these new Gentile believers and commanding them to be more Jewish. I have encountered people who, when witnessing to Jews, have the attitude of, "Well, I guess you guys can come in, as long as you are willing to accept our Messiah." In the early Church, those roles were reversed. Jesus and His disciples, along with most of the early Church, were all Jewish. So, after a number of years, as the Gospel spread, there were Jews who in essence were saying to the Gentiles, "Well, I guess you guys can come in, as long as you accept our Messiah. He was a Jew, you know, so if you want God to really accept you, you're going to have to be more Jewish."

These Judaizers then began to tell the new believers that if they really wanted to please God, they would need to be circumcised, keep the temple laws, and do all the rest of what they, the Jews, had been taught made one acceptable. When Paul heard about it, he hit the roof. "You were getting along so well," he says. *"Who has held you back from following the truth? It certainly isn't God, for He is the one who called you to freedom"* (Gal. 5:7-8 NLT). Though Paul was clearly upset, he didn't blame the Galatians, he blamed the Judaizers. The Galatian Christians were just trying to please God! They wanted so badly to be good believers that they were willing to do whatever they needed in order to receive all that God had for them. They really, really wanted to stop doing the things that their old sinful nature desired. So Paul gives them a way to get where they want to go without taking on the burden of the Old Covenant: walk in (or by) the Spirit.

JUST HOW MANY NATURES DO I HAVE?

Before we can go on to understand how to walk in the Spirit, thereby living in a constant state of revival, we need to understand what the Bible teaches about our true nature.

For many years we have taught (or at least caught) that as Christians, we now have a new nature that God plopped down into us right next to the old one that we were born with. The illustrations have been myriad. We have gone to great lengths to prove how easy it is for us to sin. Like this, used in countless sermons: "You never have to call little Johnny in from playing for Sin Lessons. Sinning comes to him naturally." It is easy for us to talk about how naturally children learn to be selfish. Even so, I still have to go back to E. Stanley Jones' idea that we are not designed to sin. We are actually designed (made in the image and likeness of God) to obey the laws and principles of the Kingdom of God.

But OK, I will concede that a person without Christ will undoubtedly, unfailingly sin. However, we have taken that to its extreme and put forth mankind's moral dilemma in terms of total depravity that make it sound as if humanity is so bad that we can do no good. There are many examples of altruism among non-Christians that negate that idea, though. Obviously, humans are capable of doing very good things. The point is not that we are as bad as we could be, but that we cannot in and of ourselves be as good as we need to be to satisfy God's requirements. No matter how many good and wonderful things we are capable of doing, we cannot redeem ourselves. We all need a Redeemer. That is the essence of the sinful nature.

So what happens to that nature when we are born again? Paul gives us a good answer in Galatians 5:24-25 (NLT):

> *Those who belong to Christ Jesus have nailed the passions and desires of their sinful nature to His cross and crucified them there. Since we are living by the Spirit, let us follow the Spirit's leading in every part of our lives.*

Romans 8 is also a wonderful discussion of the difference between the old, sinful nature and the new, God-pleasing nature. The problem is that, depending on your own personal bias when approaching these passages, it might look like a constant war is going on between the two. Here is where we need to ask God to correct the prescription of our lenses. We all have lenses through which we approach Scripture, and there is a good chance that if we are reading through the same lenses we were handed in our second grade Sunday School class, we could probably use an upgrade.

For me, the presupposed truth often went something like this: "Inside of you there is a big, white dog (new nature) and a big, black dog (sin nature), and they are constantly fighting. And the one that wins is the one you feed the most." So if I listen to a secular song on the radio, my sin nature grows stronger; but if instead I sing a hymn, my new nature is revitalized to continue the fight.

Now it is absolutely true that my inner self is helped more by "How Great Is Our God" than it is by "I Wanna Rock and Roll All Night (and Party Every Day)." No question. The issue that messes us up, though, is the whole idea of a fight. The truth of the Bible is that my old nature is dead! It can't fight. My natural force of sin has been crucified and done away with. So why do I still sin? Because I want to. Before the Holy Spirit took up residence in me, the only nature I had was a force for sin. I could not keep from sinning. Now that I have been born again, my sin nature has been killed, and I now—by my very nature—want to please God. If I still sin, it is simply because I know how to do it and I choose it willingly.

If we continue to choose to live in the way of our old, sinful nature, then yes, there will be a constant struggle.

The sinful nature loves to do evil, which is just the opposite of what the Holy Spirit wants. And the Spirit gives us desires that are the opposite of what the sinful nature desires (Galatians 5:17a NLT).

So Paul is telling us that there are two ways for a Christian to live: (1) You can believe that your old nature has power to control you, and try to defeat it through religion or struggle, or (2) You can believe that there is a higher way to live where you choose as directed by the Holy Spirit.

THE TRUTH ABOUT YOUR INHERITANCE

In verses 19-21 of Galatians 5, Paul goes on to list the characteristics of a life that is lived at the level of the old nature: sexual immorality, eagerness for lustful pleasure, idolatry, jealousy, anger, and many more. Then he says, *"Let me tell you again, as I have before, that anyone living that sort of life will not inherit the Kingdom of God"* (Gal. 5:21b NLT). I realized not long ago that I have always read that verse wrongly. Every time. Here's how I interpreted verse 21: Let me tell you again, as I have before, that anyone living that sort of life will not go to Heaven.

But that isn't what it says, is it? When do you inherit something? When you die? No! When the benefactor dies. Who died to give you the Kingdom? Jesus, of course. So when should you get it? Right now!

OK, so here it is: Whoever chooses to live the way his old, now nonexistent, sin nature taught him to live, will experience constant struggle and will not get in on the benefits and blessings of the Kingdom of God that are available to him right now. But whoever chooses to live at the level of Holy Spirit-directed decisions will experience, naturally, the fruit of walking by the Spirit: *"…love, joy, peace, patience, kindness, goodness, faithfulness, gentleness, and self-control. There is no law against these things"* (Gal. 5:22-23 NLT). Just like the Galatians, people are still looking to the comfortable parameters of performance found in religion to deliver them from the desires of their sinful nature. Kingdom living says that the old nature was crucified, so it can't help you. So walk in the Spirit, and you will get the result that you thought religion was going to give you.

THAT'S ALL GREAT, BUT WHAT DOES IT *LOOK* LIKE?

A good friend and mentor of mine, Peter Parris, says that the bishop in the Middle Ages who divided the Scriptures into chapters and verses did us no favors. Before then, if you wanted to find a certain passage, you had to read before it and after it, and you automatically got the context. Similarly, the place where chapter 6 starts in Galatians may not be the best. We can begin to understand a little of what walking in the Spirit looks like if we take out the division and start with Galatians chapter 5, verse 25.

Here, Paul encourages us to *"follow the* [Holy] *Spirit's leading in every part of our lives."* Then, starting in verse 26, he begins to illustrate it: *"Let us not become conceited, or provoke one another, or be jealous of one another."* That's what it looks like to walk in the Spirit. But he doesn't stop there. In Galatians 6:1, Paul says that walking in the Spirit involves stronger Christians rescuing brothers and sisters who have been overcome by sin. Verse 2 tells us to share each other's troubles and problems. He even refers back to their attempts at keeping the law: *"Share each other's burdens* [troubles and problems], ***and in this way obey the law of Christ"*** (Gal. 6:2 NLT). In verses 3 through 10, Paul continues to give examples of what Holy Spirit-led living looks like.

I have found that the best way to understand what walking in the Spirit looks like is with the acronym ARK. ARK can help us learn how to walk in the Spirit and make Kingdom-directed choices all day long.

"A" stands for "Antennas Up." This speaks of being aware that there is an invisible realm around us that is more real than the one we see with our eyes. I could have made the "A" stand for "Aware," but that's not nearly as fun a word as "Antennas." We ask the Lord to make us constantly aware that the Kingdom of God is here, and we seek to stay tuned in to that frequency.

A few years ago, I decided that I would try to pray for at least three people every day. Not the prayer-list-in-my-notebook kind of prayer, but the "right there with them, out loud wherever we are" kind. I hadn't made much headway when I took my then 8-year-old Nathaniel to his first soccer practice. As I was standing with the other parents, chatting, I overheard another mom and dad talking about their younger daughter, who was 6. I had noticed her feet and legs as she ran around, and saw that they were covered with painful-looking welts and splotches. I found out that she had psoriasis on her hands and feet, as well as grass allergies and a peanut allergy. Before we left, I sidled over to her parents, introduced myself, and asked if I could pray for her. "Yes!" they said, "that would be great! Thank you!" So Nathaniel and I laid our hands on her on the soccer field and we prayed for the Kingdom of God to come and be manifest in her. In the space of that one-minute prayer, I noticed that all of the stress I had been dealing with that day just melted away. I knew then that what I wanted to do all day was just pray for sick people wherever I could find them.

So I began to wonder where could I find sick people? And, obviously, the answer came to me: Hospitals are full of them! I would start there. A few days later, a woman in my church asked me to visit her sister in the hospital, which I was glad to do, because she would be number one for the day. I went to her room, visited with her, and prayed with her. As I left her room, I stopped at the room next door and interrupted a nice older man during his breathing treatment. "Hello," I said, "I'm a local pastor, and I'm here just praying for people. Can I pray for you?"

"I guess so," he wheezed. So I walked in and prayed for the Kingdom of God to be manifest in his body. As I was leaving the ward, I saw another man in another room, and asked him the same thing. He agreed, and I went in to pray for him. As I was walking back to my car, I thought, *Well, that was easy!* I had hit the jackpot.

The next day, I went back. This time, though, I figured I might as well start with those most in need, so I proceeded directly to the Intensive Care Unit. Out of courtesy, I mentioned to one of the nurses behind the desk who I was, and that I would be going into all the patient's rooms and praying for them. The look of quiet fear in her eyes should have tipped me off. I got through two rooms when another nurse, rather larger than the first, approached me smiling and asked if I was related to the patient. I said no, that I was just praying silently for the people there. She went on to tell me that I couldn't do that because families had certain preferences about religious visitors. I thought about telling her that I wasn't really religious, but decided that the nuance might be lost on her.

So I was effectively thrown out of the hospital for praying for people. Now what? "Lord," I prayed, "You're just going to have to bring them to me. Bring me sick and needy people and I promise to pray for them." The very next day, my wife and I were having lunch at a local diner when BAM, two cars collided right outside. We looked and saw steam rising from the vehicle, people staggering. My wife said, "Do you think you should go help?"

"I guess I should," I said, trying to make it sound like I thought of it first. I ran across the street to two older women who were struggling to get out of their just-mangled car. The van that hit them at the traffic light was now on fire, and the carpet installers who were driving it were frantically trying to carry huge rolls of sculpted shag to the side of the road before it went up in a chemical conflagration.

"They tried to kill us!" one lady was exclaiming. I was pretty sure the van driver wasn't trying to kill anyone, but I could tell that this was not a time to try and bring patience and understanding to their world. I spoke softly to her, tried to calm her, told her I was a pastor in case that helped (it didn't), and stayed with her until the ambulance came. After a while, my work was done, so I trotted back to my fried oyster sandwich. I related all I had seen to my wife, and then, a few minutes later, as we drove from the parking lot, it hit me—I didn't pray for anybody. Not once. I even told them I was a pastor and didn't pray for them. I slapped myself in the head to get my antenna working again.

Two days later, I stopped by my house in the early afternoon to change clothes for an appointment. I had been praying in the car, "God, please bring me someone to pray for today." While I was home, my in-laws came in, a bit panicked. My father-in-law had just had a drastic drop in blood sugar at a restaurant in my neighborhood, and they stopped at my house and asked if they could stay for a while for

him to recuperate and get some sugar in him. "Absolutely," I
said, "take all the time you need! Can I get you anything?"
No, they said, they didn't think so. So I went back to my
room, and as I was changing shirts, I resumed my prayer:
"Please, God!" I cried. "Please bring me someone to pray
for!" I don't know if you have ever felt quite as dense as I did
that day, but I had asked the Lord to make it so obvious to
me that even I wouldn't be able to miss it, so He took me
up on it. As I am coming out of my room, my mother-in-
law said, "Mark, before you go, could you pray for Milton?"
Again, I slapped myself. "Of course I will." So I prayed for
him, was happy to do it, and the presence of God was manifest in that room.

The point is, it might take you a while to recognize when
your antennae are actually picking up a signal, but keep trying,
and eventually God will make it so that you have to trip over
them to miss your opportunity.

MEANWHILE, BACK AT THE ARK

OK, back to the ARK. "R" stands for "Respond in the
Moment." As you just saw from my own experience, you may
not always hit it at first, but the more you see, the more you will
step out and respond. But sometimes you won't.

It was late on a Friday afternoon, and I was at the bank to
deposit my paycheck. As expected, the line was long, so I quietly
took my place and waited. Before long, though, my attention
was drawn, along with everyone else's, to the elderly man a few

people in front of me. He was loud. And staggering. And kind of strange. It was all a little unnerving. But he wasn't drunk. He was explaining to the man behind him, at full volume, leaning like the Tower of Pisa, that he had neuropathy, which made his feet numb. That, he said, was why he couldn't drive. As he talked and staggered, he would grab toward whatever was close to steady himself. I couldn't help but notice the uneasy looks that the customers were giving each other, as if to say, "Can you believe this guy? Maybe if we ignore him, he will just go away."

I knew better than to join that kind of thinking, so I stared right back at them as if to say, "How dare you be so uncomfortable around someone just because he has a medical problem. What if that were you, or someone you love? He can't help it, and it's very rude of you to be so…well, rude!" I'm sure they got all that from the millisecond-long expression on my face. As I watched him, I even thought, *I should pray for him, right now.*

The problem is, I didn't. I am not proud of that. The reason I didn't pray for him was because, in spite of my righteous indignation at the others, I was embarrassed by him. I didn't pray for him because all the other bank customers would think I was as weird as he was. This didn't all go through my head at the time, but as I drove away, I knew the truth.

But there are others who are responding in the moment. One night, my 13-year-old son, Samuel, asked if he could have a few friends for a sleepover on Friday night. I am rarely excited about Samuel's sleepovers because, though his friends are wonderful young men, I know it's going to be loud and they are going to eat a lot, for hours. But Samuel is a great kid, so I said yes. Then he said, "You know something I want to do during the sleepover?"

"What?" I asked.

"I want to have a prayer meeting." Now, I have been to lots of prayer meetings in my life, and judging by my experiences, I felt a warning was in order. Then again, if prayer meetings did for them what they had done for me so many times, they would be asleep in no time.

"That's great," I said, "but don't be discouraged if it doesn't go well."

"Why wouldn't it go well?" It was at this point that I realized I was discouraging my own son from gathering his friends to meet with God. I decided to repent.

"Maybe I can help a little," I offered. "If you would like me to help you put together a little prayer guide you guys can use, I will be glad to. How long do you plan on praying?"

"We're going to shoot for half an hour." Put most 13-year-old boys in a prayer meeting late at night, and they won't make it over three minutes. Still, I encouraged him.

"I'm really proud of you, son. I think it's a great idea."

I wondered if they would really do it, but at one point on Friday night, I noticed that the video game noises had stopped. I walked through the living room, and there were four teenage boys, sitting on the floor, reading Bible verses to one another and talking about what they had meant to them lately. I was overwhelmed by the sense of the presence of God in that room. I believe when 13-year-old boys get together at a sleepover, open their Bibles, and get on their knees, Heaven takes notice. I asked Samuel the next day if they prayed for half and hour. "No," he said. "It was more like an hour and a half." They responded in the moment to the reality of the Kingdom of God among them.

ON EARTH AS IN HEAVEN

And last, the "K" in ARK stands for "Klaim the Prize!" No, I'm kidding. Actually, the "K" stands for "Kingdom Come Praying." I love how Bill Johnson, pastor of Bethel Church in Redding, California, explains that according to Jesus' Model Prayer, there are really only two parts to prayer: worship, and praying for the Kingdom to come. So as we walk in the Spirit, we are aware of the reality of the Kingdom—we respond to that reality in the moment, and we pray that God's rule and reign, His Kingdom, will be made manifest in that situation.

When I pray this, I think of Play-Doh®. Here's why: Have you ever seen those Play-Doh® machines where you put something in it then bring the handle down and squish it? The handle is actually a mold, and it presses itself onto the lump of clay, and the lump suddenly looks like the design inside the mold. That is Kingdom come praying. It is asking God to superimpose His Kingdom, His rule and reign, onto whatever situation we are responding to. We want that situation—that job, marriage, child, sickness—to look like it would look in Heaven. That's what Jesus meant when He said, *"On earth as it is in heaven"*(Matt. 6:10).

On December 4, 2011, the church I pastor held another Gas Buydown. This is a servant evangelism event where we, in cooperation with a local gas station, buy the price of gasoline down 20 cents per gallon for two hours. During the two hours, we have the opportunity to pump gas, wash windshields, give out bottled water and soft drinks, and pray for dozens and dozens of people.

On this particular day, as my wife was asking one of the customers how we could pray for her, the woman said that we could pray for her niece, who was suffering serious symptoms of juvenile rheumatoid arthritis. The little girl had gone blind in her left eye. My wife quickly motioned me over when she realized that the niece was right there in the car, and we immediately began to pray "Kingdom come prayers" for her. And there, in a gas station parking lot, on a Saturday afternoon, that 8-year old girl received her sight in her blind left eye! So responding to the reality of the Kingdom is simply constantly praying for God's will—again, His rule and reign, His Kingdom—to invade our reality and change it to look like His.

Now imagine what that would look like. If every Christian were to live at this level of Kingdom reality, the world would be experiencing God Himself, and we would be experiencing something that we could very easily call revival.

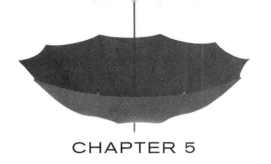

CHAPTER 5

SO JUST WHERE WAS WALDO?

Back in the mid-1990s, my children were the perfect age for the *Where's Waldo?* books. They drove me nuts. Waldo frustrated the daylights out of me. Why can't the man just stay in one place? And why the cane? It also occurs to me that no one has been looking for Waldo for a while. Maybe he got himself a GPS unit. Anyway, my kids loved the books. They would sift through tiny person upon tiny person, page after mind-numbing page until they found the lanky geek in the red-striped sweater and a knit cap. And I have to admit, I was right there beside them, trying to act like I wasn't really interested in finding him myself. But there was an undeniable thrill of accomplishment when you finally found him. It was the squeal of "There he is!" followed immediately by "Why didn't I see him before?"

In Matthew 6:33, Jesus said that we were to *"seek first the kingdom."* He didn't even say "seek revival," but rather, "seek the kingdom." I always assumed that meant to seek first "the things of God." I thought I should read a ministry book instead of a novel, listen to Christian music, not secular. The problem is that I was equating the Church with the Kingdom, but the Church is most definitely not the Kingdom. The Church is an agent of the Kingdom, but the Kingdom of God is much bigger than the Church. The Kingdom exists and even flourishes in places the Church has never been. I have personally heard missionaries to Muslim populations tell of Jesus appearing to Muslims before the Gospel ever reached them so that when they heard about Him, they already knew who He was. And they tell me that this is happening over and over! So, to *"seek first the kingdom"* has nothing to do with being enveloped in a Christian atmosphere.

So what did Jesus mean?

When Jesus said to seek the Kingdom, He was saying this: just look for it. Look for it everywhere. When I am seeking something, it is usually not a casual glance around. If I have lost my car keys or my wallet or my sense of purpose, I get what some women refer to as "purse panic" when they realize their purse is not where it is supposed to be. Sometimes I get "purpose panic" when I have to stop and focus on what my life is actually to be about. But even when I am seeking something as small as my keys, I find myself in seeker mode until they are located. You know how some people say, "It's always in the last place you look"? Well, of course it is! Who's going to keep looking after that?

If you happen to be around me when one of these panic sessions begins, you can immediately tell the value of the object I have lost by the level of desperation in my eyes. If it's a pen that I have lost, you will hardly know it, I'll be so calm. If it's my iPhone, there'd better be a sedative and a defibrillator standing by. If it's one of my children, I'll be somewhere in the middle— OK, not really, but you get the idea. Depending on what I have lost, my level of seeking adjusts itself accordingly.

This should give us some indication of just how valuable the Kingdom of God is to us. How desperately are we seeking to find and experience the rule and reign of God in every area of our lives? How closely are we trying to find where the Kingdom of God is active right now in politics, economics, entertainment, education, and in the family? Just how frantically are we chasing after, looking for, the manifested reality of the invisible in every moment of every day?

SEEING THE INVISIBLE

Do you remember the Magic Eye pictures, or stereograms, of the mid-1990s? Out of the blue, American culture was pasted with pictures of multicolored waves and squiggles that were supposed to reveal a certain image if you looked at it correctly. These mysterious pictures were everywhere, from wall calendars to greeting cards, and it was impossible to look away, even if you weren't getting it. I remember the overwhelming frustration of standing next to someone, both of us frowning, staring, cocking our heads like puppies, when the other person shouts, "I see it!" That made me so mad! Where was it? What did the person see? And, inevitably, when you asked how he or she saw it, the response would be, "Uh…I don't know." "Relax your eyes." "Focus." "Don't focus." "Look through the paper." Well, great help you are.

I will always remember, though, the day that I got it. I was pastoring a small church in Flower Mound, a suburb in the North Dallas area, when my parents had come for a visit. I was in the middle of being intrigued by these stereograms, so I went to the bookstore and bought a calendar full of them. My Dad and I sat and stared, crossed our eyes, drooled a little, and all of a sudden, we began to see a 3-D picture emerge from that mass of swirling shapes and colors. Then, once we saw it, we could see it every time. What's more, we could look at the next one and see it right away! It was amazing! I had never felt such a wave of accomplishment and intelligence in my life.

It quickly dawned on us, though, that my wife and my mother hadn't gotten the hang of it yet. That was going to be a problem. Dad and I decided to go to a hockey game. That was the strategy that had the best chance of preserving both our marriages. Fortunately, before we left for the game, my mother saw it. Dad relaxed. My blood pressure rose. My wife is a wonderful, wonderful woman, but I knew that if she remained the only one not able to see the special picture, none of us would sleep.

I hardly enjoyed the hockey game. I kept hoping that the puck would be slap-shot in my direction, knock me out, and I would wake from a coma days later to find that my wife had seen the pictures. I was still nervous when we slipped in the front door and heard laughter and easy conversation coming from the living room. She had seen it! The abundant life would continue in our home unabated!

I had that same feeling when I began to see the reality, immediacy, and presence of the Kingdom of God and what it could mean for my life. The first three letters of "seek" spell the word "see," and when you begin to *see* the Kingdom of God and its relevance and importance for every day, something that was hidden begins to emerge. This truth of the Kingdom has been there ever since Jesus first announced it, but it has become hidden to us, in the background, lost amid the confusion of what we *think* we see.

But what would a stereogram be if no one told you that there was more? What if all you saw was a flat mass of swirls, waves, and colors, but you didn't know that there was something of substance hidden in it, something that wasn't just part of it, but actually defined its existence? If you didn't know there was a bigger picture in the very fabric of the image, placed there by design, by the hand of its creator, you might try to understand and interpret the image based on your own knowledge and experience with art. But you would be missing it. You might even be able to appreciate the colorful artistry and even teach people what you think it means, but you would be wrong. The purpose of the stereogram is not to impress you with color or design, it is to show you something deeper, something that was there the whole time; you just had to be told to look for it. That's why Jesus said, "The Kingdom of God is here." That's why He said to look for it.

If we approach life, the Bible, even Christianity with a shallow appreciation, not knowing that there is more to what we are seeing, we can miss the one thing that was placed there by design, the one thing we were actually meant to see—the rule and reign of God every day, in every area of life.

SMELLING THE BREAD OF REVIVAL

In Matthew 13:33 (NLT), Jesus gives us an interesting picture of the "hiddenness" of the Kingdom: *"Jesus also used this illustration: 'The Kingdom of Heaven is like the yeast a woman used in making bread. Even though she put only a little yeast in three measures of flour, it permeated every part of the dough.'"* Now, to understand this parable, we have to get away from the Old Testament idea that yeast, or leaven, always represents sin.

In the Passover, there is a part of the feast when the father removes the last bit of leaven from the house, symbolizing repentance and the removal of sin. Even in the Old Testament, though, leaven doesn't always mean sin. When the Israelites were set free from Egypt, the only reason they took unleavened bread was because they needed to move quickly, and leavened bread would not have time to rise. So leaving out the equation of yeast and sin, what does this parable mean?

A biotech website defines yeast as "A general term for single-celled fungi that reproduce by budding."[12] Sounds kind of like a seed, doesn't it? To put this in context, in the very same chapter where Jesus compares the Kingdom to yeast, He also calls it a mustard seed that, though small, grows into the largest of garden plants (see Matt. 13:32-33). Still in the same chapter, He says that in the parable of the sower and the seed, the seed is the message about the kingdom. Later still in chapter 13, Jesus calls the *"sons of the kingdom"* the good seed. Jesus is obviously drawing us a word picture here, trying to get us to see the Kingdom as a force with a life all its own that starts small and grows.

I remember when I was a boy and my mother would make homemade bread. This was way before the days of the bread machine, so she did it all by hand and it would take hours. My mother would mix the flour and add the yeast and other ingredients to make the dough. She would knead it over and over with her petite, but skilled, hands, and then she would put it in a loaf pan and cover it with a dish towel. This was always the most fascinating part for me. Over the next few hours, that small lump of dough, left all alone, would rise and grow until it was ready to be baked. I loved seeing the effect of some invisible force in that lump of dough. Once my mother mixed the yeast in with everything else, it became invisible. And yet, every corner, every slice, every crumb of that loaf of bread had been changed by a little bit of yeast.

Yesterday morning, I stopped by Krispy Kreme® on my way to church. This was purely for research purposes, you understand. At the Krispy Kreme® close to my house (too close, actually) I can watch the whole doughnut-making process from start to cholesterol. I can watch the baker mix the dough in a huge vat, pull off some of the lump, make it into a small white ring, and place it on a conveyor belt. This belt is actually a series of trays that then slowly travel up and down in a heated glass cabinet, where the "nut" (like nuts and bolts) made of dough (dough-nut) will rise and be ready to be flipped into a trough of hot grease. After being flipped again in the grease to cook the other side, the doughnut travels through a "waterfall" of pure sugar glaze that I like to call the Curtain of Death. At this point, when the red neon light that says "Hot Doughnuts Now" starts buzzing, all notions of calories and consequences just drift away into oblivion, and this magnificent wonder of sugar-coated fried bread becomes a thing of beauty and a source of goodness and light. Wow. I'll be right back.

As I stood nose-to-glass watching this process take place yesterday, I noticed that although not every doughnut emerged from the heated cabinet perfectly formed, every last one of them, without exception, rose. The yeast, though a small amount, had permeated every bit of the large lump of dough. This, then, is the truth of the Kingdom of God. It may be hidden, but it's working.

And the Kingdom is working in every area of life. You may not see it yet, but it is there, inside the very being of the world, changing it from the inside out, causing it to rise, to be different, so that one day, when Jesus returns, we will present to Him the changed and sanctified kingdoms of this world. We will join with Heaven, proclaiming that, "*The kingdom of the world has become the [kingdom] of our Lord and of His Messiah, and He will reign forever and ever!*" (Rev. 11:15b).

NO SUCH THING AS LOUD YEAST

Have you ever had to close your ears because the sound of bread rising was so annoying? This is another aspect of the hiddenness of the rule and reign of God: You may not detect any movement with your ears, but those little yeast particles are having a major party. In his classic work on the Kingdom published in 1899 George Dana Boardman writes:

> How unobtrusively and noiselessly the leavening process goes on in our kitchens. True, there is intense chemical activity and vigorous molecular movement throughout the entire mass; but not a sound betrays the working of the transforming energy. The cook may put her ear by the rising dough; but the dough will be as still as silence itself. Even so it is with the leaven of the Kingdom. The Kingdom of God comes not with observation: neither will they say, Lo here! Or There! For lo, the Kingdom of God is unfolding among you and within you. Recall the parable of the Unfolding Seed. The real forces of Christianity work, so to speak, underground. Our King carries on his Kingdom, not superficially, but subterraneanly. What he asks is not area of surface, but depth of soil, knowing full well that length of root means breadth of tree and wealth of fruit.[13]

There is always a time of waiting while yeast multiplies itself, or while a seed in the ground dies, breaks open, and germinates. But, living in 21st century United States of America, it is extremely difficult for us to wait blindly. We want to know something is happening! And when we don't hear something happening, we assume that nothing is happening. But when it comes to the transforming power of Christ in our lives, nothing could be further from the truth. Trust God's rule and reign to work in you, even if you don't feel any different. Know that the nature of the Kingdom of God is that it works in you noiselessly.

One more thing about this: Remember that it works in other people just as noiselessly. In other words, shouting at your husband until he changes isn't going to help the rule and reign of God unfold any faster in his life. Constantly berating your children for their bad choices will not make the development of the character of Christ quicken its pace. By the same token, though, I firmly believe that Christians should be involved in changing the world around us—it doesn't happen by screaming at it. I doubt there has ever been a demon of hell that was intimidated by the volume of a Christian's voice. I believe this is what James is talking about when he writes, *"My dearly loved brothers, understand this: everyone must be quick to hear, slow to speak, and slow to anger, for man's anger does not accomplish God's righteousness"* (James 1:19-20).

REMEMBER THE BLOB!

When I was in grade school, my favorite time of day was 3:30 in the afternoon. School let out at 3, and sure, that was great, too, but 30 minutes later was when The Big Show with

Max Goodman started. On Channel 5, every day, Monday through Friday, Max brought me a movie. Every now and then he would throw in something I had absolutely no interest in, like a crime drama of some kind, but mostly it was Abbot and Costello or The Three Stooges. Sometimes, though, my brothers and I could thrill for the next 90 minutes to great '50s sci-fi like *The Crawling Hand,* or *The Giant Gila Monster,* or maybe even *Killer Shrews.* Boy, those were the days. Mom knew that on those days, either we would need Salisbury Steak TV dinners on a tray, or she would have to wait until 5 o'clock if she wanted us to eat with the rest of the family.

The most special of all days, though, would be when The Big Show featured *The Blob,* starring a young Steve McQueen. It was years before we knew that he had actually gone on to do anything else. For us, *The Blob* remained the pinnacle, the reference point, of his career. I remember watching *The Blob* and seeing people running, screaming from the movie theater, trying to escape a giant mass of grape jelly. *Why?* I wondered. What's so scary about that thing?

Well, after I grew up, I understood how horrifying it would be to be run over by an out-of-control gelatin salad, and I knew that I would have run screaming, too. The problem with the blob was that they couldn't stop it. It just kept coming. It came under doors, it broke out of compartments, it oozed through windows and ventilation shafts. OK, now follow me here: To me, the blob was a giant lump of alien bread dough on steroids. This is what leavened bread does; it keeps going, spreading and overtaking, multiplying itself in whatever vessel it finds itself.

George Dana Boardman refers to this aspect of the rule and reign of God in saying that it works "pervasively":

> It is true of each son of the Kingdom. Observe how the leaven of the *evangel* (the good news) gradually assimilates to itself the whole moral nature—choice, will, reason, imagination, conscience, impulse, habit, plan, every capacity, bringing every thought, feeling, love, aspiration, into captivity to the obedience of Christ. Thus it leavens the entire man—spirit and soul and body. And it is also true of society at large. The heavenly leaven passes from heart to heart, leavening every heart it truly touches. This leavening process is at work today beneath the surface of society on a scale which the world and even the church little imagine.[14]

This is good news for all who want to see their lives totally and consistently changed by the presence of God. If you want to live a revived life, you need to know that the Kingdom of God, His rule and reign, will work in you just as God has designed it to work until you are fully affected, every part of you, by the power of His presence. It will break down walls that you don't even know exist in your heart. It will break through preconceptions, ungodly belief systems, hurts and wounds, doubt and distrust. This life force of God that we call the Kingdom will overtake you if you let it, and it won't be like being swallowed up by the blob; it will change you from the inside out until every part of your heart looks like Jesus.

Again, remember that the Kingdom works the same way in the hearts of others, too. If you feel frustrated because you have been praying for the rule and reign of God to overtake your wife's short temper and cause her to be more patient, then wait quietly and trust that the Kingdom of God is like leaven. If you find yourself thinking that this Kingdom thing must not be real because your husband still has trust issues, do not despair. This Kingdom will overflow all of his compartments and overtake his whole being, too—if he allows it.

One more really wonderful thing about yeast: It does what it does completely apart from human intervention. Once my mother mixed her bread dough, she did absolutely nothing to make the dough rise. Once those little white rings of not-yet Krispy Kremes® went into that warm cabinet, the next person to touch them was me...um, I mean the customer. The employees had nothing to do with the dough rising. That was the job of the yeast.

The Kingdom of God is working; and frankly, it will go on working and achieving the goals of God even if we decide not to be involved in changing the situations and lives of ourselves and those around us. The wonderful thing about the Kingdom, though, is that God has invited us to be part of a process that He is ultimately responsible for! We get to enjoy the working of the Kingdom, even though He has done all the work.

TRAGEDY AT KRISPY KREME

As I watched this remarkable process take place at the Krispy Kreme®, I have to tell you that I saw one thing that saddened my heart. At the end of the conveyor belt, after the prettiest doughnuts have been plucked up and put lovingly into boxes and bags, the others—the rejects—are left to slide off the rollers and make the long plunge into the waste basket. I watch this, and everything in me wants to shout, "No! Stop the madness! I'll take it! I don't care what it looks like, it'll taste the same!" But, since I know such behavior would be frowned upon, I hold in my protest, and a tear slides silently down my cheek.

Now for the good news: In the Kingdom of God, not one iota of the love of God goes to waste. As you seek the Kingdom, God is not watching to make sure you "do it right" every time. He isn't evaluating how pretty or appetizing your life may look to others. He just wants to know that your life has been affected completely by His rule and reign. Besides, we aren't told to *look* at the Lord and see that He is good. We are told to *taste* Him.[15] So the question is not, "How good do you look?" but "How good do you taste?"

When people get a taste of your life, do they taste the Kingdom? Do people enjoy being around you because they catch a whiff of the aroma of the goodness of God's rule and reign in your life?

Remember, there are no rejects in the Kingdom. Only risen ones.

CHAPTER 6

THE *OTHER* KIND OF YEAST

Jesus also spoke of another kind of yeast that was not so good. In Matthew 16, Jesus has a face-off with the Pharisees and the Sadducees in verses 1-3. Then, in verse 5, He gets into a boat with the disciples and proceeds to cross to the other shore:

The disciples reached the other shore, and they had forgotten to take bread. Then Jesus told them, "Watch out and beware of the yeast of the Pharisees and Sadducees." And they discussed among themselves, "We didn't bring any bread." Aware of this, Jesus said, "You of little faith! Why are you discussing among yourselves that you do not have bread? Don't you understand yet? Don't you remember the five loaves for the 5,000 and how many baskets you collected? Or the seven loaves for the 4,000 and how

many large baskets you collected? Why is it you don't
understand that when I told you, 'Beware of the yeast
of the Pharisees and Sadducees,' it wasn't about bread?"
(Matthew 16:5-11)

Now, I have little doubt that I would have been as dense as
these guys, but can't you just see Jesus shaking His head as He
said this? The disciples realized that they had forgotten to bring
bread; they thought Jesus was mad at them, and I'm sure the
blame was thrown around freely.

"John, I thought you were getting the bread. Where is it?"

"Me? I told James to get it. Where's the bread, James?"

"What are you asking me for? I thought that was Bartholomew's job! What happened, Bartholomew?"

"Hey, I tried, but Judas wouldn't give me the money for it."

I can see Jesus watching all of this take place before He
breaks in and says, "OK, time out. You are completely missing the point. I was still thinking about the earlier run-in with
the Pharisees, and when you started talking about bread, it
reminded Me of the whole yeast thing. So watch out for the
yeast of the Pharisees and the Sadducees."

Matthew 16:12 tells us, *"Then they understood that He did*
not tell them to beware of the yeast in bread, but of the teaching of
the Pharisees and Sadducees."

So the question becomes, what made Jesus relate the teaching of the Pharisees and Sadducees to yeast? I think it was the

same thing that made Him relate the Kingdom of God to yeast in Matthew 13. Jesus was trying to tell His disciples that if they are not on guard against their teaching, that it would be pervasive and hidden and would do its work in them, just like the Kingdom.

But what exactly was the teaching that He was warning them away from?

If you Google® "leaven of the Pharisees," you will get a listing of about 138,000 webpages. These writers apply "the leaven of the Pharisees" to almost everyone with whom they disagree, from the Roman Catholic Church to Joel Osteen and Lakewood Church. Many, though, focus a little more closely on the doctrinal issues of Jesus' day. Most of these assert that the leaven of the Pharisees and Sadducees is the teaching that right standing with God is gained by strict adherence to the Old Testament Law. They argue that Jesus was telling His disciples not to listen to them, because they were advocating salvation by works.

Although that may be what the Pharisees and Sadducees were teaching, I do not think that is to what Jesus was referring. When Jesus referred to their teaching as yeast, He was drawing an intentional comparison to Kingdom yeast. So, if the good yeast is the Kingdom, the bad yeast must be anti-Kingdom.

Let's look briefly at the good yeast first.

As we have already seen, the good yeast is "the message of the Kingdom." So what was the message about the Kingdom?

It was simply this: "The Kingdom of God is here." Though John and Jesus both said it, their message was very different. (See Matthew 3:2; Mark 1:14-15.) George Eldon Ladd, evangelical New Testament scholar, explains it this way:

> However similar the wording may be, modern scholarship acknowledges a fundamental difference between the two messages. As we have already seen, Gunther Bornkamm recognizes that between John and Jesus 'there is a difference like that between the eleventh and twelfth hours. For Jesus calls: the shift in the aeons is here, the kingdom of God is already dawning.... It is happening now in Jesus' words and deeds. Such a conclusion is not to be determined from the terminology alone but from a study of its meaning against the total message and ministry of Jesus.... Jesus did not merely proclaim, as did John, the imminence of divine visitation; he asserted that this visitation was in actual progress, that God was already visiting his people. The hope of the prophets was being fulfilled.[16]

It is clear, then, that Jesus' primary sermon was the message of the Kingdom, and His message was that the Kingdom had arrived, and was now present and working among humanity. It follows, then, that an anti-Kingdom message must have been that the Kingdom of God had *not* arrived, and was *not* present and working among people. But how do we know that this is what the Pharisees were teaching?

KINGDOM COME

By the time Jesus stepped onto the scene, the Judaism of the day had become essentially an extension of the age of the exilic prophets like Hosea, Amos, and Joel. In other words, they were still waiting for the Day of the Lord to come and restore the people of God to their rightful place as rulers. The religious leaders of the day saw history and eschatology (the end of all things) in the same sweeping view because they were still looking through the lenses of the prophets. Since God hadn't spoken in hundreds of years, this was the most up-to-date prescription available to them. Consequently, they saw the Kingdom the way they had been taught—as something that would arrive at the end of history and would be ushered in by cataclysmic change—earth burned up, moon turned to blood, violent shaking, that sort of thing. They equated the coming of the Kingdom with the judgment of the earth. As mentioned previously, here's why…

All through Israel's history, the reputation of the people of God had been tainted by repeated sin. They would obey the Law, wander into sin and follow the gods of other nations, be judged, repent, and blessings would follow. They would live rightly for a while, sin again, be judged again, repent, and be blessed again. On and on this went, until finally, they were sent by God into Babylonian exile, where they repented once more. The only problem was, this time, blessing didn't follow right away. So they had to reevaluate the prophetic Scriptures about the Kingdom. Obviously, it didn't mean what they thought it meant. George Eldon Ladd explains how the hope of the Kingdom became a matter of eschatology, or put off until the end of time:

> This prophetic hope was not realized. The return of the Jews to Palestine from Babylon did not produce the Kingdom of God. Instead of God's rule, Israel suffered the rule of one evil nation after another. This led to despair for the coming of the Kingdom within history. History appeared to be so dominated by evil that it could no longer be thought of as the scene of God's Kingdom. Therefore the prophetic hope for an earthly kingdom within history was displaced by the apocalyptic hope of a kingdom beyond history.[17]

So for the Jews of Jesus' day, they knew that Jesus' message of "the kingdom of God is here" could not be true because no cataclysm had accompanied it. What's more, Israel was still being ruled by Rome. How could the Kingdom of God be present when Israel was still subservient to another nation?

This situationally defined interpretation of the prophets is also what gave the Pharisees and Sadducees such fervor in their teaching that the Law should be strictly observed. The expectation of the apocalyptic, cataclysmic arrival of the Kingdom was never higher, so the incentive to live right, and therefore be ready to enter the Kingdom, was never stronger. And, to their credit, they were really good at teaching it, just not so good at actually living it.

Accordingly, Jesus gives us another way to know that the "leaven of the Pharisees" did not refer to their doctrine:

Then Jesus spoke to the crowds and to His disciples: "The scribes and the Pharisees are seated in the chair of Moses. Therefore do whatever they tell you and observe [it]. But don't do what they do, because they don't practice what they teach" (Matthew 23:1-3).

Why would Jesus tell everyone to obey the Pharisees' teaching, then condemn it as leaven? Besides, in Mark's account of the warning against leaven, Jesus actually throws King Herod in there, too: *"Then He commanded them: 'Watch out! Beware of the yeast of the Pharisees and the yeast of Herod'"* (Mark 8:15). Herod wasn't a teacher of the Law, but he did have a vested interest in a kingdom other than God's.

Now, we can't leave this idea of the leaven of the Pharisees without also considering Luke's account:

In these circumstances, a crowd of many thousands came together, so that they were trampling on one another. He began to say to His disciples first: "Be on your guard against the yeast of the Pharisees, which is hypocrisy" (Luke 12:1).

If that verse is taken by itself, it might seem that the purpose of Jesus coming to earth was to tell people not to be hypocrites. But we see all through the Gospels that His message wasn't just "to thine own self be true." (That was Shakespeare, by the way, even though it sounds like King James English.) In fact, as we will see later, Jesus Himself told His reason for coming, and it was all about bringing and demonstrating the Kingdom of God.

It makes sense, though, for us to see the Pharisees' hypocrisy in light of an anti-Kingdom message. The Pharisees and Sadducees, as well as Herod, had spent years building their own kingdoms. If they were to abandon the kingdoms into which they had invested their whole lives, money, and reputation for some simple preacher from Galilee, it would mean that everything they had thought and believed and convinced others to believe would be obsolete. So, in order to hold on to their kingdoms, they had to manipulate the system, even the Scriptures, to prop up their own little worlds. Isn't that, at its essence, what hypocrisy is? Isn't it saying one thing and doing another so that your carefully constructed world doesn't come crashing down?

The Pharisees and Sadducees had been preaching the glory of the coming Kingdom of God. Now it had come, and they were rejecting it. That is the biggest hypocrisy of all. Jesus even called them on this very point:

> But woe to you, scribes and Pharisees, hypocrites! You lock up the kingdom of heaven from people. For you don't go in, and you don't allow those entering to go in (Matthew 23:13).

The religious leaders, including Herod, were trying to manipulate the masses so that they could keep their kingdoms. For the Pharisees and Sadducees, it was the kingdom of the temple system that their lives were built around. For Herod, it was his own political kingdom and his own comfortable lifestyle. In just a few years, though, it would all come crashing down anyway. When Jerusalem is sacked in A.D. 70, those kingdoms are brought to a crashing end. So because they valued their own kingdom above the Kingdom of God, they lost them both.

THE VOICE OF AUTHORITY

In describing Jesus' teaching ministry, Mark tells us that as Jesus spoke, "*The people were amazed at His teaching, for He taught with real authority—quite unlike the teachers of religious law*" (Mark 1:22 NLT). In reading this verse, for years I always pictured in my mind Jesus speaking firmly while the teachers of religious law were mealy-mouthed and wishy-washy. Now I realize that wasn't the difference at all. The Bible doesn't tell us that it was Jesus' delivery that had authority, but as it is said in other translations, His message. I am quite sure that the Pharisees and the scribes spoke very authoritatively. Surely they taught with conviction and strength as they commanded the people to obey the law in every way. So it wasn't a new style of public speaking that astonished Jesus' listeners, it was His message.

And what was His message? The Kingdom of God is here. As we have already seen, that was quite different from what the teachers of religious law were saying, which was the Kingdom of God is *not* here.

This is proved further in verse 27 of the same chapter in Mark. After Jesus casts the demons out of a man in the synagogue:

Then they were all amazed, so they began to argue with one another, saying, "What is this? A new teaching with authority! He commands even the unclean spirits, and they obey Him" (Mark 1:27).

The authority of His message was being demonstrated by His actions. When Jesus said that the Kingdom, the rule and reign of God, had arrived, they all saw that He was right when He delivered people, or healed people, or even forgave them. My friend Jack Taylor says that what starts as information becomes, by the Holy Spirit, revelation. But it doesn't stop there. As we seek the reality and the presence of the Kingdom of God among us, revelation then becomes demonstration. The demonstration of the Kingdom was the evidence of the authority and accuracy of Jesus' message. When the people saw that, the scribes could say whatever they wanted about the Kingdom *not* being there, but it didn't matter. The Kingdom was among them.

SO THIS RELATES TO REVIVAL HOW?

The point of all this is, like it or not, one of these messages is working like yeast in you right now. You are either accepting that the Kingdom of God is here and you can actually live and walk in it every day, or you are buying into an anti-Kingdom message that says it can't really be that simple, and you still have to keep your life between whatever religious lines are painted on the road.

But if you want revival—if you want to breathe the air of the Kingdom right now, not waiting until the end of time— then you can embrace the Kingdom and trust that it will do its work in you, even if you can't see it. And to continue in revival living, you must reject any thinking that says the Kingdom is not here, and that the only way you can get in on it when it *does* come is to live their way. Basically, those systems of thought— whether found in people, churches, denominations, or religious factions—are like kidnappers: "We have the Kingdom. If you ever want to see it alive, do whatever we say. Obey our instructions to the letter or the deal is off."

I have good news for you. Nobody holds the Kingdom of God hostage. Nobody owns it. The Kingdom of God is here, and it is the biggest thing on the planet. And Jesus came to give it to you, free of charge. In fact, He bought it just for you. A wonderful life in the continual atmosphere of the loving rule and reign of Father God is here for you, right now.

Go ahead and start enjoying a revived life. Give Jesus what He bought and paid for.

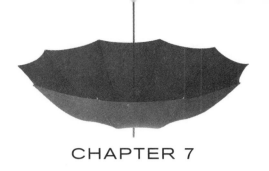

CHAPTER 7

DON'T FENCE ME IN

While we are exposing the non-Kingdom mindsets of the Pharisees, it is important to see something that they were very good at: compartmentalization. Not that it's a good thing, though. In fact, this is another area of their expertise that rightly drew Jesus' scathing glare.

Probably the number one complaint about Christians is hypocrisy. It is a very strong word, but it is trotted out with a certain vehemence every time a believer does something in a way contrary to what he has said he believes. When Ted Haggard fell publicly in November 2006, the word "hypocrite" was flung about wildly on thousands of Internet posts over the next few weeks. The word "sin" was rarely mentioned, and almost no one talked about the all-too-often reality of an honest struggle. But a lot of people were outraged that Ted Haggard apparently said one thing while doing another. The problem is that in 21st century America, calling someone a hypocrite is meant to be offensive, not descriptive. It packs too great of an emotional punch to be used casually, but, in reality, it's a pretty good word to use if we want to talk about how a person gets to the point where his intentions and actions don't match up.

The Merriam-Webster Online Dictionary defines *critic* as "one who expresses a reasoned opinion on any matter especially involving a judgment of its value, truth, righteousness, beauty, or technique." Also in our culture, to be critical means to be negative, but a movie critic can be very positive about a movie. A food critic can love a certain dish or restaurant. That's because to be a critic means to critique, or to analyze and make a judgment about something. Couple that with the Latin prefix *hypo*, which means "under," and you have someone who "under-judges" or "under-reasons."

A hypocrite, then, is a person who is not evaluating, or judging, his own life sufficiently to keep it in balance with the truth and intent of Scripture. It doesn't have anything to do with maliciously flaunting biblical principles out of sheer rebellion, but rather allowing one's heart and mind to be deceived about the contradiction between his words or beliefs and his actions. Often, it involves some sort of contorted interpretation of Scripture in order to resolve the initial conflict in his heart and justify himself.

This is why Jesus was so accurate in calling the scribes and Pharisees hypocrites in passages like Matthew 23:13. I'm fairly sure that no Pharisee got up in the morning, looked in the mirror, and said, "All right, here we go! I am going to work very hard at keeping people out of the Kingdom of God today! Woohoo!" In fact, probably every Pharisee thought he was doing all the people a favor by being so hard on them. So how could they be so harsh when God, even as revealed in the Old Testament that they knew so well, is a God of mercy to His people? What kept them from seeing that their lives were in opposition to the heart of God? One word: compartmentalization.

Jesus addressed this issue with the Pharisees in Matthew 12. He was passing through the grain fields on the Sabbath, and His disciples were hungry, so they began to pick and eat some heads of grain. The Pharisees saw it and got very upset (there's a shocker) and accused them of breaking the Sabbath by "working."

> *He* [Jesus] *said to them, "Haven't you read what David did when he and those who were with him were hungry—how he entered the house of God, and they ate the sacred bread, which is not lawful for him or for those with him to eat, but only for the priests? Or haven't you read in the Law that on Sabbath days the priests in the temple violate the Sabbath and are innocent? But I tell you that something greater than the temple is here! If you had known what this means: I desire mercy and not sacrifice, you would not have condemned the innocent. For the Son of Man is Lord of the Sabbath"* (Matthew 12:3-8).

Then, in the very next scene, the Pharisees, trying once again to trap Him, asked Him if it was lawful to heal on the Sabbath while He was looking at a man with a paralyzed hand. This, of course, was a trick question. They knew Jesus healed wherever He went, and they knew His views of the Sabbath. So after Jesus again explains that the Law of God is subservient to the heart of God, He heals the man's hand, and *"the Pharisees went out and plotted against Him, how they might destroy Him"* (Matt. 12:14).

Why were they so upset this time? Because Jesus was systematically and effectively breaking down the carefully constructed walls that they had built around their hypocrisy. The Jews at that time were all about two things: the land and the temple. Threaten either of those, and big trouble lay ahead for you. Jesus knew this perfectly and probably chuckled a little inside every time He talked about the destruction of the temple or the insignificance of where people worship. So when He said that something greater than the temple was already there, the Pharisees just could not handle the truth.

But what exactly did Jesus mean? Was He talking about Himself? I don't think so, for two reasons. First, He said "some*thing* greater than the temple is here," not some*one*. Also, if you look elsewhere, Jesus affirmed His divinity, but He never referred to Himself as "greater than." Why would He? There was never a need for Him to compare Himself to anyone or anything else. What did Jesus constantly say was "here"? The Kingdom of God. So then Jesus is saying that the Kingdom is greater than the temple. The rule of God is bigger than the house. Bill Johnson says it well in his book *Dreaming With God:* "While God will not violate His Word, He often violates our understanding of His Word. Remember, God is bigger than His Book. The Bible does not contain God; it *reveals* Him."[18]

So in the Kingdom of God, the Son of God is bigger than the day of God. In the Kingdom of God, every day is holy because Jesus has redeemed all of our days, not one-seventh of them. Jesus, as God's firstfruit sacrifice, made all of our money holy to Him, to be used for the glory of God, not just one tenth. In the same way, He has sanctified our whole life, making every day holy before Him. This is where compartmentalization comes in.

The Pharisees violently fought for the integrity and sanctity of the Sabbath, and they held up that day as holy, but they were under-critical. No matter how well they adhered to the letter of that Law, no matter how they sacrificed themselves to obey, Jesus said that God would rather have them show mercy to people every day than have their complete outward obedience once a week.

> *If you had known what this means: I desire mercy and not sacrifice, you would not have condemned the innocent. For the Son of Man is Lord of the Sabbath* (Matthew 12:7-8).

The point is that if we are to live in and experience the reality of the Kingdom of God in us and among us right now, we have to let this Kingdom destroy the compartments that we have built for ourselves. No more lines between sacred and secular, no more being respectful on Sunday and full of hell the rest of the week. Remember Blue Laws? These were city ordinances that prohibited the sale of beer and wine on Sundays because it would offend God. "Wait a minute," you might say, "isn't that a good thing?" It is, only in the sense that it is evidence that something in us knows that we are supposed to live holy lives, but religion has taught us that it's OK to limit that holiness to an outward show of respectability one day a week.

Even the world came to see the incongruity—the hypocrisy—when the Blue Laws were changed to say that beer and wine could not be sold on Sunday...before noon. I mean, what's the difference? Saturday, Sunday, Thursday—if something offends God on Sunday, why would it not offend Him on Monday or on Tuesday evening, or at 9:14 on Friday morning? God is not impressed with a polite nod on Sunday morning and our solemn promise that we won't buy a beer before noon. He *is* impressed, though, with a heart that seeks to know Him and live for Him every day, and every moment of every day.

Remember *The Blob* discussed earlier? Watch the movie again sometime and see if it respected compartments. No! It oozed through vents, it burst through glass doors, it blobbed under walls, around corners—it could not be stopped! That is the Kingdom of God. George Dana Boardman says it like this:

> It is true of each son of the Kingdom. Observe how the leaven of the *evangel* gradually assimilates to itself the whole moral nature—choice, will, reason, imagination,

conscience, impulse, habit, plan, every capacity, bringing every thought, feeling, love, aspiration, into captivity to the obedience of Christ. Thus it leavens the entire man—spirit, soul, and body.[19]

As we have been learning about the Kingdom at the church where I pastor, one of the questions that has come up is, "How does the Kingdom work in my home? If all this is so real, why is my husband (or wife, or son, etc.) still so angry (or depressed, or anxious, etc.) at home? Why isn't the Kingdom working there?" The answer is that it *is* at work in your home, even if you can't observe it yet; and it will *continue* to work until every area is taken over by it—if we continue to seek it. We cannot give up on praying for God's Kingdom, His complete rule and reign to come, and for His will to be done in every area of our lives, churches, families, and our cities. Every time we pray it, the Kingdom advances a little more. When we ask for His Kingdom to come, His answer is never no.

And, as our friend Jack Taylor teaches, the Greek tense in The Lord's Prayer of Matthew 6 is *aorist,* which means "right now, at this moment." Jesus is not instructing us to ask for something far off in someday, but for the rule and reign of God to be superimposed on the life of our husband's, or wife's, or son's anger, or depression, or anxiety *right now!* And He always says yes to that prayer. So trust the nature of the Kingdom and watch for the bread to rise.

BUT WAIT, IT GETS BETTER

So this is our hope: that the Kingdom of God, His reign, will be extended beyond all borders and will not only affect, but take over every area of human endeavor. A pipe dream? If it were anything other than the rule and reign of God, I would agree. If we were looking for human philanthropy, education, or wealth to have that kind of persistent and pervasive power, we would be disappointed in short order. Other world religions may also poise themselves to take over, but if they are not born of the Kingdom of God, they are doomed to fail in the face of a superior rule. Hear George Dana Boardman again on this subject of the pervasiveness of the Kingdom:

> It is true of society at large. The heavenly leaven passes from heart to heart, leavening every heart it truly touches. This leavening process is at work today beneath the surface of society on a scale which the world and even the church little imagine... Never in the history of Christendom has the leaven of the Kingdom been so thoroughly assimilating and trans-figuring the world's moralities, business, politics, opinions, customs, civilization, as today. The King's leaven is in the world; and you can no more stay its graciously fermenting process than you can expunge the name of King Jesus from the page of history, or annihilate his immortality. Messiah's triumph is an inevitably assured certainty, not only because it has been decreed in the counsels of eternity, but also because His Kingdom is like leaven. Jesus Christ is

the true bread from heaven, which, fermenting in human society, is raising human society heavenward. Mankind will be the new lump, because Jesus Christ is himself the leaven.[20]

In Daniel chapter 2, when Daniel interprets the dream of Nebuchadnezzar, he explains that the king's dream of a multifaceted statue represents kingdoms of the world, past and present. In the dream, a rock breaks off of a mountain, crushes every part of the statue, and grows into a mountain that fills the whole earth. Here is the last part of Daniel's interpretation:

> *In the days of those kings, the God of heaven will set up a kingdom that will never be destroyed, and this kingdom will not be left to another people. It will crush all these kingdoms and bring them to an end, but will itself endure forever. You saw a stone break off from the mountain without a hand touching it, and it crushed the iron, bronze, fired clay, silver, and gold. The great God has told the king what will happen in the future. The dream is true, and its interpretation certain* (Daniel 2:44-45).

The Kingdom of God that displaces your fear and depression is the same Kingdom that will do the same thing for people all around the earth. The rule and reign of God that heals your body is the same rule and reign that is healing people all around the earth. One thing is certain: The Kingdom will work in your home because the Kingdom works. There is no way that it *cannot* work. It is pervasive, it is redemptive, and it is the biggest thing going on Planet Earth.

How can you trust that this will happen? You can trust the Kingdom to work because of one thing—you can trust the King. Isaiah said it like this:

> *The dominion will be vast, and its prosperity will never end. He will reign on the throne of David and over his kingdom, to establish and sustain it with justice and righteousness from now on and forever. The zeal of the LORD of hosts will accomplish this* (Isaiah 9:7).

So, then, there is an absoluteness, if you will, about the Kingdom of God. There is a sense of its unstoppable success in which we can place our confidence. Let me paint you a picture in the next chapter of how that came about.

CHAPTER 8

OVERRULED

What does it mean that God's Kingdom rules over all? In order to explore this concept further, we will look at two verses from Psalms, and then we'll think about the big story of God's rule and reign. Here are the Scriptures from Psalms:

> *The LORD has established His throne in heaven, and His kingdom rules over all* (Psalm 103:19).

> *For You have upheld my just cause; You are seated on Your throne as a righteous judge* (Psalm 9:4).

Even before the earth was created, God ruled over all. He ruled over the universe, both the material and spiritual, visible and invisible. His throne had been established in Heaven, and He reigned in love and joy over all the heavenly realm.

Then God, in an overflow of His loving reign, created the earth and all that is in it. He created humankind, a being who could enjoy Him as much as He enjoys being Him. But He would not force this race of beings to love Him because love must be given, it cannot be programmed or demanded. So He gave man a will with which to choose, so that when he chose to love God, it would satisfy the longing of both their hearts.

God, in His loving rule, put these first people in a garden where all of their needs would be met, and where He would walk with them in the cool of the day, talking with them, revealing Himself, sharing life together. Then He did something that could only come from a King who loves—He gave them dominion. He gave them the authority to rule the earth on His behalf, to govern it as an outpost of His heavenly Kingdom, to represent on earth what life with God is like, what life is like in Heaven.

So man ruled the earth. He gave names to God's creation, and he governed as a reflection of Him in whose very image he had been created. Until one day when into this perfect order, disorder slithered in. Satan, whose own attempt to overthrow the throne of Heaven had failed miserably, had found that God's throne had been established too firmly to derail His rule in Heaven. But maybe, just maybe, these pitiful little creatures that He loved so much, maybe they could be recruited, or at least used as pawns to disrupt and destroy the rule of God in this colony of Heaven, this stage called Earth.

And so satan dangled the fruit of anarchy, the deceptive promise of self-rule in front of these lesser versions of God Himself, and they took the fruit, and consumed it. And rebellion seeped into their very being, deep into their fiber, so deep that all those who came after them would be infected by it. But along with this imprisoning freedom came guilt, shame, and remorse, things they were never intended by God to feel.

Then came the missing. They began to miss God, and He missed them; but their rebellion had created a great rift between them. A gaping hole was felt in the depth of their souls, because when you abuse and reject the greatest love in the universe, you feel the greatest hurt in the universe.

And now God, operating by His own Kingdom laws, having given man stewardship, or management, of the earth, did not take that management back. When He gave it to man, He gave man the right to lay it down. God never gave away ownership of the earth, but He watched the right to govern it slip away, given by man's sin to whomever they obeyed. And satan, for the first time, earned the title "god of this world." And his plan to undermine the throne of God from a distance was set in motion.

The Bible tells us that when satan tempted Jesus in the wilderness, he showed Jesus all the kingdoms of this world and offered to give them over if Jesus would bow down and worship him. Jesus did not argue with satan about his ability to give kingdoms. Satan, because of man's failure to govern the earth with the mind of God, had seized his moment and illegally picked up the authority that Adam had laid down through sin. Never one to recognize boundaries, satan had acted as usurper once again. Because the earth and everything in it had been born from a spiritual world, because the spiritual realm came first, rulership of earth must emanate from a spiritual base, and now that rulership had changed hands. No longer would the world and its systems be a colony of Heaven. Now it would become an outpost of hell.

A DAY IN COURT

How can it be, then, that the psalmist can say with such confidence that the Lord has established His throne in Heaven, and that He rules over all? In order to find the answer, we look at Job chapter 1, where we get a glimpse of the courts of Heaven. On a day, the Bible says, that the angels came to present themselves before God, satan came with them. In that scene, we see how he conducts himself before God, and we see him in the role that John would later hear proclaimed in Heaven itself, "*the accuser of our brothers*" (Rev. 12:10). So, in the heavenly court, where God sits as the one righteous Judge, there is one who comes before Him "day and night," as John tell us, to accuse the people whom God loves so much.

Surely satan came to court the day he received the deed to this world and its systems. He would have strutted, with all the pride that condemned him, to the very throne of God, and, seeing the infinite, boundless love with which God still reached out to Adam, said, "Objection! This experiment of Yours has failed! Those insignificant, worthless lumps of flesh and bone have betrayed You. They have ignored Your command, they have scoffed at Your love and have chosen themselves over You. They have decided that they want to know what You know, to be like You, to ascend to the throne of the Most High! When I did that, You cast me out of Heaven. Now, I demand that they be cast out of the heaven You have made for them. In the matter of man's right to rule the earth, I object!"

And there was silence in Heaven. When the Father spoke, He did so with a calmness and confidence that belied the words He said next, as if He was looking further ahead than anyone else could dream. "Objection sustained," He said. The angels gasped, and satan chuckled in self-satisfaction, but the Father just watched.

And so God, to keep man from eating from the Tree of Life and living forever in his fallen state, "drove man out," the Bible tells us, *"east of the garden of Eden He stationed cherubim with a flaming, whirling sword to guard the way to the tree of life"* (Gen. 3:24).

Yet God continued to reach out to His beloved creation, loving them, wanting to forgive them. And when satan saw that God still loved man, he marched into the court of God, and cried out, louder than before, "Objection! You know the law! Anyone who rebels against You must be punished! Sin is, as we all know, the highest crime against the highest holiness, and it is punishable by the highest penalty. When I rebelled, You took away everything I held dear, and now I demand justice in the heavens. You must take away what he holds most dear—life! And since You have given them blood to make them live, I demand blood for their crime. If You are really holy, if You are really just, then I object! Blood must be shed!"

And the Father held His breath...then, slowly, He nodded. "Objection...sustained," He said.

But God, whose loving-kindness was reaching out to man, found a way to shed innocent blood and still spare these people whom He loved so much. And so God slew animals, and it was the first time that anything, anywhere died. And He took the skins of the animals and gave them to man to cover his shame and guilt. And the precedent became law, a law that could never be repealed—sin is punishable by death. Where there is sin, blood must be shed. It is the only payment fitting the offense.

And so, all through the ages, as God continued to reach out to man in unbounded love, calling him back, extending mercy and compassion to him from generation to generation, satan continued to parade himself before the courts of Heaven, day and night, accusing and attacking at every turn. When the earth was filled with unrighteousness and wickedness prevailed in every place, satan saw God's patience and cried, "I object!"

I OBJECT!

"Sustained," said the one righteous Judge, and a flood covered the earth. But Noah found favor in the eyes of the Lord, and so came a new beginning.

But again, sin reigned in the human race under the iron hand of hell, under whose rule the earth moaned. So when the people of God followed after idols, satan raised his fist and yelled, "I object! They don't deserve Your favor!"

"Sustained," said the Father, and off they went into slavery or exile, while the Father kept reaching.

And when Saul, the anointed king of God's people, rebelled against the commands of God and chose his own way, the now familiar "Objection!" rang again from the voice of the accuser. "He doesn't deserve to lead Your people!"

"Sustained," agreed the Father, and a new king was found, one whose heart chased after God's own heart.

And when David succumbed to the pull of temptation, the voice was heard: "Objection! You say he has a heart like Yours? Ha! He is an adulterer and a murderer. How dare You let him build Your house. I object!"

And the Father, even while forgiving David's sin, seemed to agree. "Sustained," He said, and the task of building a temple to the name of the Lord was passed to the next generation.

But there was a mystery, as yet unrevealed, working its way down through the passage of time. God had a plan. It was a plan that He had always known would be put into motion, a plan to redeem, to buy back what man had lost. This plan unfolded behind the scenes, quietly but powerfully. The prophets would speak of this plan to send a Savior, a Messiah, someone who would restore everything to its proper order. The people of God heard the promise, and they waited, and watched, all the while under the constant accusations of hell.

Then one night in a pasture outside of the little town of Bethlehem, this plan of God that had been hidden in the ages burst out into the open. "Rejoice!" went up the cry, as all the angels of heaven packed themselves into a tiny piece of sky and sang the song that they had been waiting thousands of years to sing. "For unto you is born, this day, in the city of David, a Savior, which is Christ the King! Rejoice! Glory to God in the highest heaven, and peace on earth to all people on whom His favor rests!" (See Luke 2:11-14.)

And for once, on that night, while all of Heaven sang at the top of its lungs, the familiar scream of objection could not be heard.

And the tables began to turn. The court of Heaven went into recess. The accuser became very busy trying to hold on to his power while the Judge spent time with His family, watching His Son grow up. Jesus grew in stature, the Bible says, and in favor with God and with man (see Luke 2:52).

At the age of 30, this Man, the Son of God, took the plan of God public. He began to attack satan's power base and train others to do the same. For this reason, John tells us, the Son of God was revealed—to destroy the works of the devil (see 1 John 3:8).

So on it went, for three and a half years, satan struggling to hold on to an authority that he sees slipping away, and Jesus, casting the kingdom of darkness out of people and replacing it with the Kingdom of God.

In a last-ditch effort to hold on to his ever more tenuous position, satan rallies his troops, and a scheme is hatched to kill his greatest threat. Using forces both inside and outside of Jesus' organization, satan succeeds in staging what is surely the most brilliant coup in the history of the world. He arranges for Jesus to be arrested, illegally tried, convicted, and sentenced to death at the hands of those He said He had come to save. Tortured, mocked, spit upon, accused, this one Man, the only Man who had never sinned, carried His own wood of execution through the city streets, up to a hill outside the city gates, where everyone could witness His shame.

And so, as all of Heaven falls silent, satan steals quietly back into the courtroom and watches as, once again, God sits down on His throne and prepares to hand down a decision. Satan, knowing he has won, strikes a pose of victory and waits for his moment, the moment when he will declare that God's greatest plan has failed, that He has lost the earth and its inhabitants forever.

But something catches satan's ear. He hears a conversation that is taking place on that hill far below. Jesus is stretched out, crucified, dying, done for, and satan hears the last part of something being said. It is coming from one of satan's own people, someone he has invested much time and energy into and then discarded. It is coming from one of the thieves hanging beside Jesus. *"Remember me,"* he is saying, *"when You come into Your kingdom"* (Luke 23:42).

And then the ancient and accursed accuser hears something that shakes him to his very core: *"I assure you: Today,"* Jesus says, *"you will be with Me in paradise"* (Luke 23:43).

"Objection!" satan screams, high-pitched and scared. "He can't do that! That man is mine! He lived a life of sin, and he belongs to me! You know the law! I object."

THE VERDICT

And the Father looks down. He sees the blood of His own perfect Son flowing down the rough, splintered wood of the cross. He sees one perfect life slipping into death, sinlessness becoming sin; and even as satan's objection echoes through the halls of Heaven, the Father stands from His throne, looks at satan with all the authority that has resided in Him since the beginning, and says, finally, the words that all of Heaven has been waiting to hear since before time began:

"OBJECTION OVERRULED! The blood of My Son is enough! It is sufficient to pay the price for all of sin, for all time!

From this day forward, no more sacrifice will be required. No more blood need be shed. All who believe on the name of the Lord Jesus Christ will be saved. Saved from the penalty of their sin! Saved from death! Saved from you! They will be the rescued, the redeemed, the righteous people of God, and we will be together both now and forever!"

"No," cried satan, his voice beginning to crack under the strain, "You can't do that! The world is mine! Remember? They gave it to me! I object!"

"OVERRULED!" shouted the Father, and the doorposts of Heaven shook. "Man gave it to you, and now the Son of Man has bought it back! He has brought My Kingdom, My rule, My reign back to the earth and its inhabitants. They no longer need to be under your darkness, living in your chains! This court hereby proclaims that by the blood of My dear Son, mankind is free!"

And far below, Jesus answers back, "It is finished!"

JESUS—THE REDEEMER

I can see satan, scurrying back to hell as fast as he can go, trying to figure out what went wrong. His argument was iron-clad, his victory sure, he thought. What happened?

No sooner does he slink into his dark, oppressive chamber, but there is a knock on the door of hell. He ignores it. But the Visitor is insistent. The knocking grows louder. "Nobody's home!" he tries, cowering in the corner. And a Voice responds, "I'm coming in anyway!"

At the next knock, the gates of hell are blasted inward as the Victor comes for His spoils. Jesus, arrayed in glory, stands at the threshold, undaunted, unafraid, the undefeated Champion. Someone is with Him. A wide-eyed young man stands behind him, mouth open, watching. Satan points a bony finger. "Who is that with You?" he asks from behind a chair. "Wait! I know him! That is the thief on the cross! Have You come to deliver him?"

Jesus smiles at the man standing behind him, then turns and says, "You must be mistaken. This man is not a thief. He *was* a thief. Now he is righteous. Now he's with Me. And, no, he has already been delivered—from you."

"Then why are You here?"

Jesus steps toward him and holds out His hand. Satan backs up, trying to hide behind the horde of demons that has come to see about the commotion. They are the same demons who last saw this Man being beaten, the same ones who laughed and prodded as the nails were driven. But now, here He is, standing in front of them, holding out one of those mighty, nail-scarred hands.

"I am here," Jesus says, in a voice that echoes through all the ages, "for the keys."

"What keys?" asks satan.

"The keys to death and hell. They don't belong to you anymore. In case you don't remember, hell was prepared for you and your angels, not for the people for whom I just died. It is true, people will always have a choice. They can choose to reject the love of My Father, reject My love, the price that I paid—and then they will share your eternity. But that is their choice. Not yours. No longer do you have power or authority over them. You have accused them unopposed for far too long. They now have an Advocate with the Father. I am now on their side."

And satan thought of what worked so well for him before. "Objection!" he screamed.

And the response rolled down from Heaven with astonishing power, "OVERRULED!"

And Jesus took the keys and walked back up, up from the bowels of hell, leading captivity captive, up into the tomb where they laid Him, and He *burst* through the other side in radiant light, *risen and alive forevermore!*

AND STILL TODAY

And still today, the father of lies tries to lie his way into the hearts of men and women. He tells them that he still rules, that there is no way out, that they are under his control. But still, God proclaims to them, in myriad ways, His great love and deliverance.

And still today the accuser appears before God day and night, bringing cases against the children of God, those who have entered into the forgiveness and cleansing of the sacrificial blood of Jesus.

"Look!" he cries, pointing. "See that one there? Did you see how he just treated that waiter? And you say he's one of Yours. I object!"

And the Father looks down from His throne, and all He sees is someone robed in the righteousness of Jesus Christ and stands forgiven by His blood. And He turns confidently and triumphantly to satan. "Overruled."

"Look!" the devil says again, "Did You see that pastor? A pastor! Look what he is involved in! And the people, YOUR people, have no idea! Surely You must give him to me! You can't keep him! I object!"

And the Father, with grief in His heart for a suffering child, still shakes His head and says, "Objection overruled. It is true that he is hurting himself with his sin, and I miss spending time with him, but he will always belong to Me. Always."

"Look there!" the devil continues. "And there! Are You blind? Can't You see their sin?"

And the Father, with the righteous anger of a daddy protecting his children from attack, stands and leans toward their accuser. "No," He says, "I don't see their sin. I see a redeemed man, I see a woman who once was dead but now is alive again.

I see a teenager who was lost, but he has been found by Me. I see a young girl confused by the world, hurt by friends, but holding on to My love for her. I see people who are struggling to live free from the chains you had them in, but they are winning. They are learning. They are growing. And I love them with all of My heart.

"Do you want to know what I see? Every time I look at them, every time they come to Me in tears and in repentance, every time they struggle, every time they fail, every time they succeed beyond their wildest dreams, do you know what I see? I see Jesus. They no longer wear the old, tattered rags that you had them in. They now wear the robe of righteousness of My Son, and His blood cleanses them from ALL sin!

"So go ahead, accuse them all you want, throw whatever indictments you can find, scream out your arguments until time is no more, until the earth and the sky disappear, until all the kingdoms of this world have been handed to Jesus and He gives them to Me. It doesn't matter. One day, when the earth has run its course, My people will finally be able to say, 'The kingdoms of this world have become the Kingdoms of our God and of His Christ!' So, until that day, know this, and know it well—every accusation, every indictment, every argument against them, every objection you can ever scream out will be met with one word: OVERRULED!"

The Lord has established His throne in heaven, and His kingdom rules over all (Psalm 103:19).

CHAPTER 9

HOW TO *REALLY* SEEK THE KINGDOM

In an earlier chapter, I mentioned briefly the difference between "seeking" and just looking around, especially within the context of seeking the Kingdom. Let me unpack that for just a moment to show you how you can know, without a doubt, that you have positioned yourself as a Kingdom-seeker every day.

To reiterate what was discussed about seeking, remember that the degree of passion with which you look for something reveals its importance to you, but let's take that a step further. There are some things in our lives that, if they are missing, not only do we look for them diligently, turning the house upside down until we find them, but very often we cannot rest until they are found.

You lie down in bed, and you tell yourself that surely the item must be around somewhere, I mean, it couldn't just get up and walk away. And yet, your eyes do not close. You toss. You turn. You get up. You put on whatever shoes you don't have to bend down to tie, and you go out to the car, in the rain, to see if it fell under the seat. In other words, real seeking will not let you rest until you find whatever you don't have. That is what it means to "seek first the Kingdom." Does just the thought of that exhaust you? Take heart. I think I can help.

PRAY LIKE THIS

But seek first the kingdom of God and His righteousness, and all these things will be provided for you (Matthew 6:33).

What things are *"all these things"*? We will get to that in just a moment, but I think we can agree that whatever "these things" are, we want them. If God has them, and He has willed them to us, bring 'em on. But that highlights the prerequisite "seeking" on which we are camping out. When Jesus tells us to *"seek first the kingdom of God and His righteousness,"* and when we realize what kind of energy is required to qualify as seeking, it begs the question, "How? How do I do that? In practical terms, what does it look like when I seek the Kingdom, and how do I know if I am doing it right?" Well, I do not intend here to say whether there is a right way or wrong way to seek the Kingdom, but I do believe that Jesus Himself gave us a way to put our obedience into concrete action in the verses just before that promise in Matthew 6:32. And as I was praying about this, it came from the unlikeliest of places—The Lord's Prayer.

What Jesus gives us in Matthew 6:9-13, though sometimes called The Lord's Prayer, is probably more accurately referred to as the Model Prayer. (Some say that the Lord's Prayer should refer to Jesus' High Priestly Prayer in John 17.) I like the phrase Model Prayer, because Jesus begins it by saying, "*You should pray like this….*" Now, before we unpack this prayer to see how to seek the Kingdom, allow me to point out the simple truth that Jesus said "pray *like* this," not "pray *this.*" Scripture memorization is a wonderful thing and should always be practiced and encouraged, but Jesus' intention was not to just memorize that prayer and repeat it every day and think that we have really prayed. (That being said, like my friend Jack Taylor, I also believe that the words of Jesus and the authority of Scripture is so full of power, that whenever that prayer is prayed, even by rote, Heaven pays attention and responds accordingly, regardless of our level of confidence in what we are saying.)

Two years ago, our oldest son, Samuel, got his driver's license. On that day, my prayer life dramatically intensified. As I was praying for him with renewed passion, I heard myself praying for protection over him like never before, as have so many millions of parents before me. As I prayed, though, something that I have been rolling around in my spirit for a couple of years finally wriggled its way to the front of my brain. What happens if I forget to pray for his protection one day? Will that be the day of a parent's worst nightmare? Will I get a blood-chilling call from the police department that day because I neglected to ask God to protect him? Or does God's protection of my family flow from His love for them and His plans for their lives? Will God really not protect them if I don't ask, or is His sovereignty bigger than my devotion and discipline?

That led me to the Model Prayer and to another series of questions: In the same way, what if I don't pray one day, "Give me this day my daily bread"? Will God not give it? And what about *"forgive us our debts"*? Isn't that already mine in the atonement of Christ? And then there is "do not bring us into temptation." Will God actually lead me into temptation if I don't ask Him *not* to do so? If all these things are true, why did Jesus say to make those requests? In order to answer all these questions, let's unpack them a little more.

GIVE US THIS DAY

Just after Jesus models prayer for us, He explains to us why we don't have to worry about our daily bread:

This is why I tell you: Don't worry about your life, what you will eat or what you will drink; or about your body, what you will wear. Isn't life more than food and the body more than clothing? Look at the birds of the sky: they don't sow or reap or gather into barns, yet your heavenly Father feeds them. Aren't you worth more than they? Can any of you add a single cubit to his height by worrying? And why do you worry about clothes? Learn how the wildflowers of the field grow: they don't labor or spin thread. Yet I tell you that not even Solomon in all his splendor was adorned like one of these! If that's how God clothes the grass of the field, which is here today and thrown into the furnace tomorrow, won't He do much more for you—you of little faith? So don't worry, saying, "What will we eat?" or "What will we drink?" or "What will we wear?" For the idolaters eagerly seek all these things, and your heavenly Father knows that you need them (Matthew 6:25-32).

If that is true (and it is), then why include the petition for daily bread? In fact, the very next verse, where Jesus spells out the benefits of seeking first the Kingdom, is meant to be a direct contrast to idolaters, Gentiles, who do worry about such things, *"The Gentiles eagerly seek these things (material needs)... but as for you, you should eagerly seek the Kingdom"* (Matt. 6:32-33, author's paraphrase). Before I explain, let's look at the implications of the other two requests in the Model Prayer.

FORGIVE US OUR DEBTS

In his letter to the Colossian church, apostle Paul uses some of the most beautiful language in all of Scripture to illustrate what Jesus accomplished in His death:

He erased the certificate of debt, with its obligations, that was against us and opposed to us, and has taken it out of the way by nailing it to the cross (Colossians 2:14).

Jesus paid our debt to God! Let's all call in to the Dave Ramsey Show and yell, "I'm debt free!" (I actually think Dave would enjoy that.) So, if our sin debt to God is paid, if our sins are forgiven—past, present, and future—so that we will never have to pay for them ourselves by being separated from God, then why do we need to pray *"forgive us our debts"*? Are we asking God to forgive our debts to other people? Isn't that their responsibility? Granted, when we walk in bitterness or unforgiveness, our fellowship with God is broken and we need to "come clean" before Him in repentance and confession. But that is about fellowship, not relationship. Because of Jesus' death on the cross, my relationship to God is, and always will be, one of sonship. Notwithstanding your view or mine on the eternal security of the believer, I think we can agree that Jesus paid our debt. No other sacrifice will ever be needed or adequate. So, if I don't pray as Jesus modeled, am I in danger of my debt being reinstated?

And how about this last one?

LEAD US NOT INTO TEMPTATION

Let's hear James on this matter:

No one undergoing a trial should say, "I am being tempted by God." For God is not tempted by evil, and He Himself doesn't tempt anyone. But each person is tempted when he is drawn away and enticed by his own evil desires (James 1:13-14).

Do we really believe that God would actively and intentionally present us with opportunity to sin? Of course not! Then why ask Him not to do so?

I believe the answer to all of these questions is found between the bookends. After an introductory confession of praise and worship, the body of the Model Prayer in Matthew 6 is bookended with two declarations that give the rest of the prayer its context—the reality and presence of the Kingdom of God among us. So in order to put the whole prayer into context, and given what we now know about the reality of the Kingdom of God, allow me to paraphrase the first part of the prayer from introduction to the first bookend.

HOLY IS YOUR NAME

Almighty God, it is so good to know You as Father. Generations past have known You only as God, yet now You are revealing Yourself as the ultimate Father through a relationship with Your Son. You, Father, reign and rule from Heaven itself, that realm in which Your glory and goodness permeate every square inch, unhindered by anything that might assert itself against Your total rule. There is no one like You; there is absolutely no other God in existence anywhere in the universe! You alone are holy; You alone are the unchallenged and unchallengeable God, reigning in authority far beyond anything anyone could ever imagine. Now, Father in Heaven, let that unimaginable realm of Your glory, that invisible reality more real than what we see, let the atmosphere and the character of Your invisible Kingdom break into our realm, and let Your rule and reign be superimposed on this world. Let Your Kingdom come! Cause the delivering and life-changing power of the realm in which You live and move and from which You deal with us so invade our realm that earth starts to look like Heaven itself because of the mighty, torrential flow of Your very life through us. Let Your decrees be obeyed, Your will be carried out, as quickly and powerfully on earth as it is in Heaven.

I don't know about you, but rewording that helps me a little bit more than just saying, *"Hallowed be Thy name"* (KJV). Maybe that's because I live in 21st century America, where the only time we use any word even close to "hallowed" is around October 31. Somehow that cultural context doesn't do much to help me reflect on the glory of God. Now on to the rest of the prayer.

THANK YOU FOR THE BREAD

Remember, we have an advantage that the original hearers of the Sermon on the Mount didn't have. We can look at the whole thing in one glance and see that part of what Jesus was doing early in Matthew 6 is setting up what He would say later in Matthew 6. Of course, *they* had the advantage of actually hearing how Jesus said all these things firsthand.

So, if Jesus was just about to drop a bombshell of a declaration about God's ability to provide for us as we seek first and only the Kingdom of God, it stands to reason that He knew when He was giving the Model Prayer, what He would be saying in a few short minutes. So if we couple seeking the Kingdom (looking everywhere until we find it) with God's promised provision, then *"Give us this day our daily bread"* (KJV) becomes something like this:

Father, in light of Your promise to provide my daily bread as part of my sonship and citizenship in Your Kingdom, I ask You to manifest Your kingship and lordship in my life by causing Your promise to manifest in my reality. Open my eyes so that I may see and recognize that You are the owner and ruler of everything in my life. I will look diligently today for You to reveal Your care for me by providing my physical, material needs. It is not a question of whether You will provide for me, Your son, but whether I will recognize that provision as Your reign and rule being made manifest in front of me, and give You thanks and glory for Your faithfulness and goodness. So Father, as concerns my daily bread that You so faithfully provide, bring it on, so I may use that occasion to proclaim the reality of Your Kingdom love for me!

Starting to get the picture? Let's keep going, and do the same thing with the next part.

RECONCILING THE BOOKS

As we have already seen in Colossians 2:14, the sacrifice and blood of Jesus was more than sufficient to wipe away the record of our sin debt to God. Our account has been paid in full. Now the Model Prayer moves from the area of our physical needs, to the arena of our relationships. Jesus connects our vertical account (Godward) with our horizontal account (manward). It is absolutely true that if we harbor unforgiveness in our hearts and refuse to give it up, our growth in God stops cold. Oh, He will certainly still talk to us, but at the top of the agenda is settling that horizontal account.

I believe that God will not continue to speak to you as if nothing has happened if you willingly hold on to bitterness. As already stated, unforgiveness is such a huge deal to God that it can break your fellowship with Him, even while your own forgiveness stands as a positional reality in Heaven. So again, if you consider your debt to God paid, and pair that with a proclamation of the Kingdom, your prayer might sound something like this:

Now, Lord, today, would You please cause my relationships with other people to reflect the grace and forgiveness that I enjoy with You because of the blood of Jesus that has paid my debt. Please remind me today of the forgiveness that I have in You, and cause me to respond to others with the same degree of love, patience, and life-changing restoration that You have shown to me. As I enjoy Your forgiveness, I will look for the manifestation of Your rule and reign in my life by actively passing on that forgiveness to anyone else who trespasses against me.

Let me say a word about that word "trespass." Depending on your age, the version of the Model Prayer that you may have memorized might have used "trespass" instead of "debt." Frankly, I kind of like the word. Here's why: Most of the offenses between people, most relationship injuries, come from trespasses.

In the Old Testament, there was a sin offering, and there was a trespass offering. The sin offering was for blatant, I-know-I'm-about-to-do-this-but-I'm-gonna-do-it-anyway kinds of sin. Intentional, premeditated, because-I-want-to sin. The trespass offering, on the other hand, was for the times when people might break one of the laws of God because they didn't know that there even was a law that covered what they did. Ignorance of the law was, in fact, an excuse of sorts, but an offering still had to be made. Now, in the New Covenant, there is no such thing as trespass sin between us and God. As James said, God does not tempt us with evil. In fact, we even have the Holy Spirit resident within us to warn us before we sin:

> *...but your Teacher will not hide Himself any longer. Your eyes will see your Teacher, and whenever you turn to the right or to the left, your ears will hear this command behind you: "This is the way. Walk in it"* (Isaiah 30:20-21).

However, I think we do still experience "trespass sins" in our relationships with other people. It's like going hunting, and walking through the woods, before you know it, someone is accusing you of trespassing on his property when you never saw the "No Trespassing" sign. It doesn't mean the sign wasn't there, but for whatever reason, you missed it. Often, when people get offended with one another, it is simply because someone crossed a line that he didn't even know was there. Obviously, there are times when someone may hurt you on purpose, but the vast majority of the time, we spend days or weeks sulking and pouting when the person who hurt us has no idea that it's going on inside of us until we can't hold it in any longer and we spit up all of our hurt on him. That person crossed a line, and now we can shoot at him.

So, let's put that idea into what we just prayed:

Father, as I enjoy Your forgiveness, I will look for the manifestation of Your rule and reign in my life by actively passing on that forgiveness to anyone else who crosses the line with me.

And last but certainly not least, there is the matter of our walk with God, or our inner life.

BUT YOU, O LORD

Apostle James could not have been more clear that God absolutely never gives us opportunity to sin. That would be counter to God's whole character and His desire for us to live in victory. So what does Jesus mean by *"lead us not into temptation, but deliver us from the evil one"* (KJV) ? Well, to see it, let's do the same thing we have done with the other elements. Let's realize what is already ours as children of God, and look for His rule to be revealed. In the arena of our inner life, or our walk with God, the prayer might be worded like this:

> Father, I thank You today that You love me so much that You have already provided for my deliverance from satan's plans against me. Thank You that You are at work constantly causing the schemes of his kingdom to bow to the purposes of Your Kingdom. I want to see Your ownership of my inner self revealed before my eyes today. Please show me how You are protecting me and delivering me from the evil one. Let me rejoice openly and with great joy, at how "You, LORD, are a shield around me, my glory, and the One who lifts up my head" (Ps. 3:3). Today, please manifest Your plans for me by defeating the plans of my enemy. You have already disarmed principalities and powers on my behalf, and I am earnestly looking today for how that is shown in my walk with You.

THE OTHER BOOKEND

See how that works? Now, for the climax of the Model Prayer, we put the whole in its context with the other bookend— another proclamation of the reality of God's Kingdom:

Now, Father, I will look for You to show Yourself and Your kingship in my life today in my physical needs, my relationships, and my walk with You. I seek Your Kingdom! I won't rest until I see how You reveal Yourself, Your plans, and Your great love for me today. I gladly undertake this discovery today because I know that it really isn't about me at all. It is all about You. My life is about Your Kingdom, Your power, and Your glory! Forever and ever! Amen!

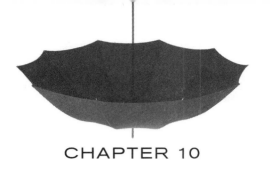

CHAPTER 10

LEANING INTO THE KINGDOM

WHAT MARY LEARNED FROM MARTHA

Pardon my indignation, but enough already. I think everybody should leave Martha alone. I am convinced that Martha, the sister of Mary and Lazarus, has gotten a bad rap in the church today. I intend to correct that forthwith. That is because Martha is one of the greatest examples that we have in Scripture of how to trust God, even when it seems like, in spite of all you know and believe and have seen from Him, God hasn't come through in the most difficult circumstance of your life. You have sought the Kingdom, and it didn't show up. Now what?

Over this next couple of chapters, we are going to tackle this thorny issue head-on. No platitudes, no placebos, no semantic acrobatics, no rewording our doctrine so that we can try and make God look good—when the fact is that our hearts have been broken, and deep down inside, we do not have an answer for where He was when we needed Him.

I hope that doesn't sound like blasphemy to you. I intend to show you that God, in fact, never fails and that He can be completely trusted. In order for us to really trust Him, though, and know that we are trusting Him completely, we have to be completely honest, both with God and with ourselves. My friend, Peter Parris, says that the question he has heard from the Lord on this matter is more along the lines of, "I know I am faithful. Now, can I trust you?" Can God trust you to trust Him? Can He freely carry out His highest Kingdom plans and know that no matter what it looks like to us at any given time in our reality, that we will not stop trusting Him with all of our hearts?

> Just how, exactly, is that accomplished? How can you know that your faith in God is real, not just some hyped-up psychological façade erected around a crumbling heart? I believe Martha has an answer.

NOT JUST ANYBODY

Now a man was sick, Lazarus, from Bethany, the village of Mary and her sister Martha (John 11:1).

Something very big is about to happen, and John begins his account of it in true storyteller fashion. "Once upon a time, in a small village, there lived a man named Lazarus...." He goes on in the next two verses to explain that this Mary who is Lazarus' sister, is the same Mary who has already had one of history's most wonderful worship experiences. This is the woman who washed Jesus' feet with her tears and dried them with her hair. (However, that has not happened yet. More about it later.) It is also the Mary who, when Jesus and the disciples came to visit, sat at His feet to listen to Him teach instead of helping her sister in the kitchen. And thereby, we get the account of Much-Maligned Martha, who obviously is too busy to listen to God—so you shouldn't be so busy either. It is absolutely true that *"one thing is needful; and Mary* [had]*chosen that good part"* (KLV). Don't let that fool you, though. We'll glance at that again in a minute.

The point is that Jesus has a well-established friendship with this trio of siblings. They hung out together. They cooked out. They played Uno. And, obviously, they had small group meetings led by the Son of God Himself. Not a bad social circle.

So, what do you do when you find out that one of your best friends is seriously ill? Call his cell phone? Rush to his side? Why would Mary and Martha expect any less from Jesus? Instead, here is what they get: *"(Jesus loved Martha, her sister, and Lazarus.) So when He heard that he* [Lazarus] *was sick, He stayed two more days in the place where He was"* (John 11:5-6). What?! Stayed? What does that mean? It means that He stayed where He was. Didn't go to the hospital. Didn't pick up and run to their sides. He did not make any moves to heal His friend. That had to be incredibly confusing to the sisters. I mean, they had to have seen Jesus heal complete strangers. Why in the world would He not heal someone He knew and loved? So they waited.

Then, after two days, Jesus told the disciples that it was time to go.

WHAT I MEANT WAS...

"Then the disciples said to Him, 'Lord, if he has fallen asleep, he will get well'" (John 11:12). This was not simply the disciples giving their armchair medical diagnosis. This statement immediately follows an interesting little discussion with Jesus about why He must be crazy to want to go back to Judea. *"'Rabbi,' the disciples told Him, 'just now the Jews tried to stone You, and You're going there again?'"* (John 11:8). They were incredulous, and more than a little afraid that Jesus was going to drag them back into the lion's den. Jesus then explains that of course they tried to stone Him. They are blind and can't see Him for the light that He is.

Basically, He is saying that the disciples should not be surprised when lost people act like lost people. *"He said this, and then He told them, 'Our friend Lazarus has fallen asleep, but I'm on My way to wake him up'"* (John 11:11). Aha! Now is their chance! Maybe they can use their extensive knowledge of sickness and healing to help Jesus know what to do here. If they can convince Him that Lazarus doesn't really need Him, maybe they won't get killed today! Here's a hint for us: We are probably not going to tell God anything He doesn't know about how to make people well.

This brings about one of the most powerful lessons of Scripture:

Jesus, however, was speaking about his death, but they thought He was speaking about natural sleep. So Jesus then told them plainly, "Lazarus has died. I'm glad for you that I wasn't there so that you may believe. But let's go to him" (John 11:13-15).

There is great comfort for us in this principle: God takes it on Himself to make His direction clear to us. If you are trying to hear God about something, and you don't think you have quite gotten it yet, He makes it His responsibility to repeat Himself until you get it. He will get clearer and simpler if He must, but He is not playing some game with you that requires you to figure out what He wants like some cosmic game of Clue. Five of the most freeing words in the Bible are, "So Jesus told them plainly...."

WHERE WERE YOU?

Jesus arrives at Bethany, the siblings' village, and we are told that Lazarus has already been in the tomb four days and that many of the Jews had come to Bethany (about two miles outside Jerusalem) to comfort Mary and Martha.

As soon as Martha heard that Jesus was coming, she went to meet Him. But Mary remained seated in the house. Then Martha said to Jesus, "Lord, if You had been here, my brother wouldn't have died" (John 11:20-21).

If we aren't careful, we want to immediately begin scolding Martha for being disrespectful. I mean, this is Jesus you're talking to, and you just don't go around talking to Him like that! The fact is, though, that Martha has just made a very true statement, at least in her mind, *If You had shown up when You were supposed to, Lazarus would still be alive.* There was absolutely no reason not to think so. We'll get back to that in a minute. What are the unasked questions in her statement? "Just where have You been? Why didn't You come? How could You let this one slip past You?"

Let's do the math for a moment. The end of John chapter 10 tells us that Jesus had left Jerusalem and gone across the Jordan to where John had been baptizing. The Jordan River is about 25 miles from Jerusalem. Walking time is about eight hours, less if you are in a hurry. Let's say the messenger who brought the news to Jesus made it in half that time. In Mary and Martha's thinking, Jesus could have made it to Bethany, to Lazarus' side, by the next day. Instead, Jesus stayed two more days at the Jordan River. Then (only being eight hours away), He doesn't show up until Lazarus had been dead for *at least* four days. By the time He shows up, by Martha's timetable, Jesus is a week late! They can't even assume He didn't get the message in time because the messenger surely came back and relayed his success in the delivery of it. So Martha's question is completely understandable: "Where have You been?!"

Be honest. Nobody's looking. Have you ever felt like that? Without any religious posturing and double-speak, have you ever, deep down somewhere in the recesses of your soul, ever seen something go from bad to dead and, even privately, said, "God, where were You?" These kinds of times are especially troubling when you know that He has heard your plea. Mary and Martha knew. In fact, Jesus responded to the news that Lazarus was sick, *"This sickness will not end in death but is for the glory of God, so that the Son of God may be glorified through it"* (John 11:4). You just know that the messenger brought *that* word back to the sisters. "Guess what! He said that this won't end in death!" Now what else could that possibly mean to Mary and Martha than Jesus would come right away.

We have the benefit of knowing how the story ends, but they didn't. They had a word from God! Woohoo! "He'll be here any minute, and He is going to fix this thing, because, well, we are the apple of His eye! We are His friends, His children, and He loves us!" And so they celebrated and confessed the faithfulness of Jesus and told everyone that Lazarus would be healed. For about two days.

Now try to imagine again what Martha might be feeling when she said, "If You had been here, my brother would not have died." I imagine she said this with red-rimmed eyes from four days of crying, through clenched teeth, and with clenched fists. She is angry, she's confused, she hasn't slept, and she is probably at least a little embarrassed that she stood up for Jesus for two days while Lazarus lay dying. But, thankfully, she went on, *"Yet even now I know that whatever You ask from God, God will give You"* (John 11:22).

I'm not sure that she even knows what she is saying, but her meaning is clear, "I don't know where You have been, and I don't know why You let us all down. There is nothing You can do about it now. But here's what I do know. I know that You know God. I know that, even now, even in my grief, You are who You said You are. I will not forget in the dark what I knew to be true in the light. I hope You have a good answer for Yourself, but even if You don't, I still know who You are. And I'm hanging on to that."

WATCH THIS!

At this point, Jesus does something spectacular. In response to her confession of reality, Jesus speaks to her the secret plan of God. *"'Your brother will rise again,' Jesus told her"* (John 11:23). When I read this, I don't hear the blond-haired, blue-eyed, sad-faced, monotone, British, Max Von Sydow, shampoo-model, movie Jesus saying this. I hear the squeaky, jumpy, I'm-about-to-burst, I-have-to-tell-somebody excitement that He has been holding in for more than four days. I think He can't wait to let somebody else in on the plan; and now Martha, by choosing to still believe in Him, has earned the right to hear it. But she doesn't hear it quite right.

"Martha said, 'I know that he will rise again in the resurrection at the last day'" (John 11:24). So here is Martha's response: "Yada yada yada, blah blah blah." She has heard this before, and probably from all the mourners hanging out at her house for the last four days. This is the equivalent to us going up to someone whose son has just died in an automobile crash and saying, "Well you know, all things work together for good for those who love God and are called according to His purpose!" Yes, it's in the Bible, and yes, we know it's true, but that is absolutely not the right thing to say in that moment. The doctrine that all Jews would be resurrected when God established His Kingdom on earth was well and widely believed, but it was always a "someday" proposition. "Don't worry, Martha," they were saying, "you'll see Lazarus again someday." Sure, that is important, but she needed her brother now.

Jesus knows she has this faulty filter of religious presupposition keeping her from understanding, and He doesn't fuss at her for this. Again, He just explains a little further. *"Jesus said to her, 'I am the resurrection and the life. The one who believes in Me, even if he dies, will live. Everyone who lives and believes in Me will never die—ever. Do you believe this?'"* (John 11:25-26). If it were me, my response to that would have been, "Believe what? What in the world did You just say to me?"

We need to note here that Jesus did not ask Martha if she *understood* what He just said. I do believe that God wants, more often than we know, for us to completely get everything He is saying to us. Sometimes, though, what is more important is that we are willing to just keep believing what we know to be true: that He is good, all the time, and He cannot be anything less. Ever.

Jesus is actually speaking directly to her faulty theology. "Yes," He says, "there is a resurrection. But it isn't someday way out in the future. The Kingdom of God is not someday out there. The Kingdom, the rule and reign of God Himself, is right here, right now, standing right in front of you. I know that might be too much for your mind to grasp today, but you'll get it later. But for now, can you just believe in Me?"

WAIT FOR IT…WAIT FOR IT

And here it comes. One of the most powerful statements of faith in all of Scripture: the one sentence that should induct Martha into the Hall of Faith in our minds for the rest of our lives. Ready? Here it is: *"Yes, Lord,' she told Him, 'I believe You are the Messiah, the Son of God, who was to come into the world'"* (John 11:27). Wow! Incredible! In the middle of the most intense suffering of her life, her darkest moment, she goes back to what she knows to be true: "I don't have a clue what You just said to me, and You still haven't told me where You were when I needed You, but here is what I know—You are still the Messiah, the Son of the Living God, the One we have been waiting for all these years."

We have to allow room for the mystery. Very often, when our circumstances don't match our theology, we change our theology to match our circumstances, and we end up living with a low view of God and His Kingdom because we have brought them down to the level of our experience. Sometimes, though, we need to resist the temptation to come up with a doctrine that explains away the truth that we already know, and allow it to be tallied in the column of "the mysteries of God."

ENTER MARY, STAGE RIGHT

Having said this, she went back and called her sister Mary, saying in private, 'The Teacher is here and is calling for you.' As soon as she heard this, she got up quickly and went to Him. Jesus had not yet come into the village but was still in the place where Martha had met Him (John 11:28-30).

Now it's Mary's turn. Before we get to her encounter, though, let's notice something. He was still in the place where Martha had met Him. Same place, same time frame, same brother, same disappointment. All things are equal to what has just taken place with Martha. The Bible says that when Mary went to meet Jesus, the people gathered with her thought she was going to weep at the tomb, so they all followed her—which, of course, was their job. Some were probably paid mourners, some were probably just friends. But whatever their role, they knew that their one job was to be a support group for the sisters. We will revisit this in a moment.

"When Mary came to where Jesus was and saw Him, she fell at His feet and told Him, 'Lord, if You had been here, my brother would not have died!'" (John 11:32). Does this sound familiar?

Isn't it word-for-word what Martha has said to Him? What does that tell you about the topic of conversation in their house over the past four days? But watch what happens next:

When Jesus saw her crying, and the Jews who had come with her crying, He was angry in His spirit and deeply moved. "Where have you put him?" He asked. "Lord," they told Him, "come and see." Jesus wept (John 11:33-35).

There it is! Jesus wept. But why?

Now, this is where people will give all kinds of reasons for Jesus' tears. One of the options is that He wept because Lazarus is already in "glory," and Jesus hated to have to call Him back from that wonderful place. I don't think so. For one thing, I think Jesus was actually stating spiritual fact when He said that Lazarus was "sleeping." Even though his body was absolutely, stone cold, doornail dead, his spirit was in a state of slumber, waiting to be called out.

Another theory is that Jesus was weeping because His friend was dead, and thus we can see that He knows exactly how we feel when we grieve over the loss of a loved one. While it is unarguably true that Jesus knows all of our pains and sorrows, we should not use this story as an example of Jesus' experience of grief. If you want to tell someone who is grieving that Jesus knows their sorrow, use the account of when He was told that His cousin and friend, John the Baptist, had been beheaded (see Matt. 14:13), but do *not* use this story! If you do, you will have to flat out ignore the whole first part where Jesus tells the disciples that death is not the end for Lazarus! How could He who planned to resurrect Lazarus from the very first minute be sad and depressed just moments before the Big Reveal?

One more thing: Weeping is not the only emotion we see here. In the verse just previous, we are told that Jesus was angry and that He was troubled in His spirit. Those feelings are more clues that give us insight into what was really troubling Him so much that He wept. He was troubled when He saw that everyone hanging out with Mary had been infected by her and were ignoring who was standing among them.

But what about Mary's statement was so spiritually debilitating? Was it what she said to Him? No, how could it be, since she said the exact same thing as Martha, and it didn't upset Him then. So what makes the difference? What made Him angry in His spirit, such that He wept? Obviously, it wasn't what Mary said. It was what she *didn't* say.

Martha was honest about her disappointment and grief, but she didn't stop there. She went on to confess her trust in who He was, regardless of what it looked like. Mary, on the other hand, in the very same situation, stopped at the point of her offense. She camped out in her hurt and confusion, and apparently forgot whatever she received while sitting at Jesus' feet the last time He was in town.

And that is where we must go now. If we are to grasp what happens next, we must go back, back to a time before all of this happened...

CHAPTER 11

THE NEW NORMAL

FROM INFORMATION
TO EXPERIENCE

Let's go back for just a moment, back to the scene where it all started:

While they were traveling, He entered a village, and a woman named Martha welcomed Him into her home. She had a sister named Mary, who also sat at the Lord's feet and was listening to what He said. But Martha was distracted by her many tasks, and she came up and asked, "Lord, don't You care that my sister has left me to serve alone? So tell her to give me a hand." The Lord answered her, "Martha, Martha, you are worried and upset about many things, but one thing is necessary. Mary has made

the right choice, and it will not be taken away from her"
(Luke 10:38-42)

Here we have the beginnings of Martha's bad reputation. Without coming to her defense yet again, though, we need to focus on Mary. Remember, all of this happened *before* Lazarus' sickness, death, and resurrection. Jesus and His disciples come to the home and proceed to hold a small group meeting. In those days, it was the woman's job to cook for any guests and serve them. Mary, though, recognizes that something of great significance is going on in her living room, so she either forgets or just ignores her social duty and sits down at Jesus' feet to listen to Him teach. So far, so good.

Martha fusses about this development, and Jesus points out to her that Mary is not in trouble, but has, in fact, made *"the right choice."* Notice that Jesus doesn't rebuke Martha for serving, just for letting herself get distracted from what is really important— His presence. Still, the score seems to be Mary 1, Martha 0.

MEANWHILE, BACK AT THE TOMB

Now let's fast forward back to John 11 and the tomb scene. Martha (the one who was too busy) has more faith in Jesus than Mary (the one who sat at His feet). How can these things be?

The simple reason is that Mary, while sitting at Jesus' feet, heard the most important words of truth ever uttered by a human being. But, at that time, it was just so much interesting information. And the fact is that information doesn't change us. It adds to our body of knowledge and may impact how we see the world, but it doesn't change us at our core. In fact, new and interesting information, especially spiritual information, tends to make us arrogant (see 1 Cor. 8:1).

All we can tell about Mary, though, is that whatever information she received at His feet, however wonderful, it wasn't enough to sustain her through the crisis. That is absolutely not a judgment on the value of the words of Jesus, but it does tell us that if good preaching were enough, then none of us would be as messed up as we actually are right now.

For us in our day, this is what I call living at "church level." There are millions of Christians who attend church faithfully every week, sing joyfully, listen appreciatively, smile warmly, love dutifully, and leave just as empty as they showed up. As the great preacher Vance Havner used to say, "We come to church at 11:00 sharp, and leave at 12:00 dull." Now, don't get me wrong. As a pastor and a Christian, I have a great love for the Body of Christ and its expression in the local church. I have given my life (many times over it seems) for the health and well-being of the local church. But again, church is so much more than the acquisition of spiritual information. It has to be. If just learning more was the answer, then why are so many Christians living in silent defeat? As has been said before, if good preaching could change the world, the world would have been changed already.

Perhaps this is one of the things that Jesus wanted people to repent of when He began to preach that the Kingdom of

God was now among us. We need to repent of thinking that just going to church consistently is the answer. I cannot tell you how many times I have counseled mothers and fathers who were either dumbfounded that their children were not living godly lives because "they are in church every week," or were firmly convinced that if they could just get their wayward children "back in church," all of those children's problems would vanish.

Church level living believes that a good church is the answer to all of society's ills. But church level thinking often doesn't see behind the curtain. It finds it difficult to hear the desperate cries for more that boil just below the skin of the happy parishioner singing right next to them. Church level mindset is content to acquire new and interesting spiritual information, file it away, and call it maturity. But when life caves in, church level living often collapses under the weight.

TAKING IT UP A NOTCH

So there is Mary, barely treading the waters of adversity and disappointment, with the truths she has collected unable to inform her about the reality of God's character. But she is about to be swept into a higher realm of living—the Kingdom level.

Let me reiterate: Information doesn't change us; experience changes us. Granted, the truths we have collected impact us, but it is only when we encounter the living, breathing power of those truths in the person of Jesus Christ and the presence of the Holy Spirit that we become changed forever.

Think for just a moment about the watershed moments of your life. Chances are better than good that the moments that have defined you were not those moments that you chose one of four possible answers on a geography test. They were probably moments when you made a choice that led you into a life experience. So how do the truths collected help us move into a Kingdom level?

Make no mistake, the role of the mind in the life of the soul is undeniable and absolutely essential.[21] But it is only in the crucible of experience that we see if the things we have heard have changed our minds enough to let the experience we are in change our hearts. And that is what Mary faces at the entrance to Lazarus' tomb.

YOU LOOK SO DIFFERENT!

So, there stands Mary, and in the next few moments, even in spite of her inability to believe what Martha continued to believe about Jesus, Mary is about to be an eyewitness to the earth-shaking, dead-raising, Heaven-come-to-earth demonstration of the power of the King and the reality of His Kingdom among them. She will watch with eyes wide open as her brother, Lazarus, is raised from the dead. And that, my friends, is the experience of the reality of the Kingdom of God that will catapult her from the church level into the Kingdom level.

Let me tell you a story of how that happened in my life. In the first part of 2006, less than three years into the life of the church I pastor, a good friend from my first church, Carolee Baugh, sent me a set of CDs that she thought I needed to hear, called "Healing: Our Neglected Birthright" by Bill Johnson. I had never heard of Bill, but I listened hungrily and I was greatly challenged and excited by the truths I heard. So, like any good pastor, I started preaching the series. I embraced the revelation. I communicated with passion. I spoke boldly of God's desire and presence to heal. I had never really seen anyone healed, at least not like Bill Johnson was describing. Still, I believed and received the interesting and important revelation, and passed it on to the people in my care.

In the winter of 2006, my heart was heavy for a man in my church, Lee McDougald. Lee was 48 years old and was dying. He had been diagnosed a few years before with a particularly aggressive form of Parkinson's Disease, and it seemed clear to everyone who knew him that he would be dead within a year. Most of the time, Lee could only walk slowly with the help of a three-footed cane, and often he would be in an electric wheel-chair. He ambled slowly, shuffling on unsure feet and wobbly legs. Lee's hands shook uncontrollably and he swallowed more than 15 Parkinson's medications daily. In light of the series I was preaching on healing, something was stirring inside of me, and my wife and I began to believe that maybe, just maybe, God could actually heal Lee.

In the middle of February, 2006, we found in the mail one day a postcard advertising a conference that we used to attend when I pastored in the Dallas, Texas, area called Amber Rose Music Conference, hosted by gifted worship leader Tom Davis.

This particular conference was called the Healing Conference, and it featured Randy Clark, Jack Taylor, and none other than the man whose series I was preaching, Bill Johnson! Also, Jack Taylor was a man whom I had listened to and admired since I was a teenager; and in fact, I already had him scheduled to come to my church in Mobile, Deeper Life Fellowship, the very next weekend after the conference was scheduled. This just sounded too right.

My wife, Mary Ann, looked at the card, looked at me, and said, with prophetic certainty, "We have to get Lee to this conference. If he can get there, God will do something!" I had no inclination to argue, but not a fraction of the conviction that she had. Still, I was ready to see what God would do. I called Lee and asked him if he would go with me if I could raise the money to get us there. Immediately he said yes. And then it started.

We quickly raised the money for airfares and one of my friends in Texas opened her home for us to stay there. Lee, however, began to experience more serious physical problems. Within a week, he was in emergency surgery, followed by a coma due to blood loss and scar tissue from a car accident 25 years earlier and resulting ailments and afflictions. He was a mess.

After about a week, he was released, still intent on going with me to the Amber Rose Healing Conference. Then, the day before we were scheduled to leave, his wife called to tell me that he had more signs of internal bleeding. Lee picked up the phone to call his doctor, knowing that as soon as he told his doctor what was happening, he would be ordered back into the hospital, which meant he would miss the conference. Lee put the phone down.

That night, he dreamed. He dreamed that Jesus was passing by, and as Lee was in the crowd, he knew that if he could just reach out and touch the hem of His robe, he would be healed. He reached out his hand and felt the robe of Jesus brush gently over his fingers. When Lee awoke, his arm was stretched out above him, his hand still reaching.

I arrived at the airport the next morning, still not sure if Lee would be going. Then, he came shuffling in, looking pale, gaunt, and moving like a man about to die. Our friend, Annette Oden, met us there with Communion, "the meal that heals," and we paused in the airport lobby, shared Communion together, and made our way to the departure gate.

Lee and I arrived at Gateway Church in Southlake, Texas, for the first night of the conference. Because of his obvious physical need, the staff allowed us to enter the room early and find our seats. Not being shy, we went directly to the second row, as close as we could get since the first row was reserved. Eventually the service began, worship started, and within a few minutes, the conference speakers all came in and sat directly in front of us! I tapped Jack Taylor on the shoulder and introduced myself, telling him that he would be in my church in Mobile the next weekend, and introduced him to Lee. Jack looked Lee in the eyes and said, with the voice of Heaven, "Lee, God is going to touch you tonight."

The worship was great and the teaching was excellent, but our expectation continued to grow, waiting for ministry time. As Bill Johnson led the ministry time, he had everyone lay hands on those around in need, as is his custom. Randy Clark, Jack Taylor, and I turned to pray for Lee. I had absolutely no faith that God would heal Lee of Parkinson's, but I did believe that He could touch and heal his recent abdominal issues. As Jack and Randy prayed, I found myself praying one thing: "God, I don't know what I'm doing. Please just don't let me mess this up."

As we prayed, I heard Bill speak to another man about how a spirit of infirmity often comes in after an accident. The Lord quickened in me that this was exactly what was going on with Lee. I relayed that information to Jack and Randy in a not-so-calm manner. I was excited! As we prayed for Lee, and as Bill made pronouncements against the spirit of infirmity from the stage, Lee began to get extremely hot, sweating through his clothes, though the room temperature was comfortable. Suddenly, he stood up tall and ramrod straight, and I knew that something had happened. He said that the pain in his abdomen was gone, and I was amazed, but not as amazed as I was about to be.

We shared that bit of news with the assembled crowd, and we all glorified God together. I thought that was it, and frankly, it would have been enough for me. But then, as we all stood for a closing prayer, Lee roughly elbowed me aside, pushed out into the aisle, stalked down to the front, and hurled his three-footed cane at the front of the stage. With a look of determination I had never seen before, he marched back to his seat; and Bill Johnson, seeing his demonstration of faith, proclaimed loudly concerning the Parkinson's, "It's over! It's over! It's over!"

And it was over. That night, we stayed at the conference until after midnight; where before, Lee would completely run out of energy at about 5 P.M. because of the medications. We laughed with our whole hearts all the way back to the home where we were staying. For the rest of the conference, Lee continued to stand straighter, walk stronger, and look happier than I had ever seen him. At that time, Lee had been taking 15 meds per day. He never took another. For a long time after, if you were with Lee for any length of time, you would hear the alarm on his cell phone go off numerous times each day. That alarm was to remind him to take the Parkinson's meds. He kept the alarms turned on. And every time they sounded, he thanked God for his healing.

By the time we had returned to Mobile, word had spread rapidly. We were having a Saturday night service then, and everyone knew that it was going to be very special. I kept Lee hidden in my office until the start of the service. As we began, I announced, "You all know that I took Lee McDougald with me to Dallas for the Amber Rose Healing Conference. Well, I brought someone different back with me." The Chris Tomlin song, "How Great Is Our God" began playing, Lee burst out of my office, and ran around the whole room again and again…

in cowboy boots, no less! As he ran, I watched the crowd. Some laughed, some applauded, some wept (including his 8-year-old daughter who had never seen her daddy run), some were dumbfounded, and some even screamed, as if terrified. Those are the kinds of reactions that you get when the reality that the Kingdom is here hits people. That's what happens when Heaven invades earth.[22]

The next week, as Jack Taylor came to preach at Deeper Life, he summed up Lee's miracle and made an indelible impression on my spirit when he said, "Let me tell you what has just happened to all of you. You have been blown into Kingdom come."

MEANWHILE, BACK AT THE TOMB

I now have a new frame of reference for what I imagine the scene to have been at Lazarus' tomb as he came out of it. I think some people laughed. I think some people wept. I think some were dumbfounded, speechless. And I think some people screamed as if terrified, because it is a terrifying thing to have the power and reality of the one true and living God demonstrated right before your eyes.

Mary has now learned one of life's important lessons: We can't un-see what we have seen. As I have heard said before, you can't un-ring a bell. Mary has now witnessed the incredible, world-changing force of the rule and reign of God, and her life cannot stay the same. Which brings us to John 12:1-3. In this scene, Jesus, some time later, passes back through Bethany on a return trip:

Six days before the Passover, Jesus came to Bethany where Lazarus was, the one Jesus had raised from the dead. So they gave a dinner for Him there; Martha was serving them, and Lazarus was one of those reclining at the table with Him. Then Mary took a pound of fragrant oil— pure and expensive nard—anointed Jesus' feet, and wiped His feet with her hair. So the house was filled with the fragrance of the oil (John 12:1-3).

First of all, notice that Martha is still serving, and no one rebukes her. Just goes to show that it wasn't "too much serving" that earned her a reprimand last time, it was the being distracted from who was actually in her house that was the problem. Let no one use Martha as an excuse to escape serving in the Body of Christ! Serving is good, it is valued, it is even necessary to be great in the Kingdom of God if you ask Jesus. This time, though, as Martha serves, she is not distracted from the importance of who she is hosting. She has seen this Man raise the dead, and now she understands that her job is to simply facilitate the presence of God.

The danger in "doing church" week in and week out is not in serving God too much, it is in serving Him and missing the importance of the One in whose presence we are serving. May God do so much stuff in our lives and ring so many bells of the bigness of His Kingdom among us that we never forget that our role is not to impress people with how well we serve. Our role is simple—facilitate the person and presence of God Himself in our house.

So where is Mary this time? Oh, she is there. Look again at John 12:2-3. Mary comes in with a full pound of fragrant oil, pure and expensive, and pours it on Jesus. Wait a minute: Martha is doing what she did last time, but with a new attitude. But Mary, oh, Mary is doing something altogether new, because she herself has been made altogether new. Mary is no longer in the mode of acquiring interesting spiritual insight. She is no longer living at church level. She has been blown into Kingdom level. Mary is now a worshiper.

So what is it that changes us from *listener* to *worshiper?* The same thing that changed Mary. Once we open our eyes to see the wonder of God at work here and now, the majesty of the King ruling in His Kingdom now, it changes us. We have to go to incredible lengths to act like we haven't seen what we have seen. It is the deep, life-changing experience with God that changes us. Information doesn't change us. Oh, information is useful, and it affects the way we see the world, but knowledge about God doesn't make us a worshiper—beholding His glory does.

> *For we did not follow cleverly contrived myths when we made known to you the power and coming of our Lord Jesus Christ; instead, we were eyewitnesses of His majesty* (2 Peter 1:16).

MAN OF THE HOUSE

One more thing before we leave this story. What exactly was it that caused Mary to choose the oil as her act of worship?

The answer is in the culture. Remember, Lazarus had died, leaving Martha and Mary as two sisters in a man-less home. In those days and in that culture, if you were a woman without a man, your career choices were limited. Basically, you could become a slave, a beggar, or a prostitute, unless you could find some benevolent relative who would allow you to move in with him, at which point you still would be treated like a slave.

When Lazarus died, that pound of ointment became the sisters' all-important life savings. It was the only thing standing between life as they knew it and abject poverty. But Jesus gave them back their brother. Even Mary, who had lost her faith, still got the benefit of the miracle. I think that Mary released the oil not just because Lazarus was alive and the bread-winner was back. No, it was much more than that. It wasn't her brother's presence in the house that was Mary's newfound security. It was her Master's.

Mary the *learner* acquired new spiritual information, but she had still only trusted in her own means of provision for security. Mary the *worshiper* knew something else. She knew that she was loved and protected under the powerful hand of the One who holds all of life. She knew that she no longer needed to trust in money, or even in herself or her loved ones. Mary now knew something that she could not un-know. She knew that the King was on His throne, and even life and death obeyed Him—and that King was sitting in her living room. Not only did He deserve all that she had to give, there was no reason to hold it back. Mary now knew what it was to trust God. She had finally moved into faith.

CHAPTER 12

SOME SAID IT THUNDERED

WHY SOME DON'T BELIEVE EVEN AFTER THEY SEE

On August 27, 2010, I watched a miracle happen again. I know there are all kinds of miracles, from the unforgettable birth of a child, to the eternal, grace-filled miracle of someone giving his heart to Jesus, which is the greatest miracle of all. I have seen both of those things, and I bow before God in thanks, but on this particular night, I saw another miracle, something I had heard about, but had never witnessed with my own eyes. On this night, I saw the lame walk. And so did hundreds of other people in the room. Since that night, over

375,000 more people have been witnesses to that same miracle through the global touch of the Internet.

On Monday, August 23, I called a friend of mine, Bishop Levy Knox, and asked if he had yet been to the meetings in downtown Mobile, Alabama, that had now been named the Bay of the Holy Spirit Revival. ("Bay of the Holy Spirit" was the original name of Mobile Bay, given by early Spanish settlers on the Gulf Coast.) Levy had just returned from a trip out of the country, and he said that he had not yet attended, though he wanted to, given a long relationship with Pastor John Kilpatrick, in whose church the meetings had begun. That same church, Church of His Presence, was now graciously hosting these citywide meetings every Thursday through Saturday evenings.

Levy said he would check with his wife, Delia, and possibly meet me there Friday. They did come, and what a meeting it was. The details of that night can be told elsewhere, but suffice it to say that before the evening was over, Delia Knox, paralyzed below the waist and wheelchair-bound for more than 22 years, got out of her chair and walked. Since that night, she has continued to gain strength, and as of this writing, a year later, she regularly ministers, on her own two feet, every Sunday with her husband at Living Word Christian Center in Mobile, and at various conferences around the country.

It just so happens that the church where I pastor, Deeper Life Fellowship, was the last church in which Delia sang before her miracle. I was finishing an eight-week sabbatical, and Levy was filling the pulpit for me that day, August 8, 2010. Delia, as she had for years, sang powerfully from her wheelchair and Levy preached a powerful message proclaiming the arrival of a new season of God's activity. He had no idea how right he would prove to be. With Levy and Delia having just been at my church, I could not wait to show the congregation the video of Delia's miracle that had been recorded the night she walked.

It was as if a bomb exploded that Sunday morning. People began asking me to post the video on the website, so on Monday morning, settled into my recliner, laptop in hand, I quickly edited and posted a 13-minute video that has now, to the best of my knowledge, been seen in every country on the planet. The video went viral immediately, spreading like wildfire in hours. But not everyone has believed what he or she has seen.

Within the next few days, other sites began embedding and featuring the video, sites that allowed viewers to comment. I had disabled the ability to make comments on my YouTube channel because I knew that Bishop Knox and Lady Delia were still awed by the power of the miracle and, together, we wanted to protect the holiness of that moment. Besides, I was in no frame of mind to deal with the critics and the naysayers whom I knew would start commenting. And so, as the video spread, and as many people around the world gave great praise to God, those who just could not believe what they were watching began to make their presence known.

No matter how much we prepare ourselves for the criticisms that inevitably come against a move of God, it always takes some time and some adjustment on our part to calm our frustrations and our natural defensiveness. As I read some of the comments about the video, one in particular struck me. "When these people cause an amputee's limbs to grow," it said, "then I'll believe." And immediately, something in my spirit responded, "No, you wouldn't. If you can't believe this, you would find some reason not to believe that."

Over the next few days, the Lord began to speak to me about where to put those kinds of statements. I knew it was real, I stood 10 feet away and watched as Delia got up out of her wheelchair. I had known her for years, I knew personally what had happened. Why could they not see?

I believe the answer to this question can be found in John 12:27-30:

"Now My soul is troubled. What should I say—Father, save Me from this hour? But that is why I came to this hour. Father, glorify Your name!" Then a voice came from heaven: "I have glorified it, and I will glorify it again!" The crowd standing there heard it and said it was thunder. Others said, "An angel has spoken to Him!" Jesus responded, "This voice came, not for Me, but for you."

This passage doesn't say that it sounded like thunder. It doesn't say that the people didn't clearly hear what God said. I believe that they heard and understood the words, but because some standing there did not have the spiritual equipment necessary to identify the realm of Heaven, they chose to rely on their own level of experience to explain it away. Since they were incapable of recognizing and admitting to the reality of the supernatural activity of God on the earth, they had to assume it was something they already understood—thunder.

When some watch a paraplegic get out of a wheelchair, or hear of God opening the eyes of a boy blind in his right eye, or even when they see the evidence of brain tumors having disappeared, or closed lungs becoming clear, they cannot even identify the activity of God because *"the god of this age has blinded the minds of the unbelievers so they cannot see the light of the gospel of the glory of Christ, who is the image of God"* (2 Cor. 4:4). If they are still *"dead in* [their] *trespasses and sins"* (Eph. 2:1), then how can they even recognize life? In other words, if we who have "eyes to see and ears to hear" are amazed and rendered speechless by the power of God, how can we rightfully expect those who don't yet know Jesus to understand? Instead, for them, it must be a hoax. The ministers must all be charlatans who are trying to fleece people and line their own pockets. It must be mass hypnosis. The ones who are walking, seeing, and breathing clearly must either be simple-minded people or paid actors. For those who don't know God, the supernatural experience they are witnessing must have some natural explanation. And so they ignore their own senses in order to make sense of what they see and hear.

In Luke 16, Jesus tells the story of Lazarus (not the one who was raised from the dead) and the Rich Man. After they both enter eternity, and the Rich Man finds himself in hell, he asks Abraham, whom he sees in Heaven, for a favor:

"Father," he said, "then I beg you to send [Lazarus] to my father's house—because I have five brothers—to warn them, so they won't also come to this place of torment." But Abraham said, "They have Moses and the prophets; they should listen to them." "No, father Abraham," he said. "But if someone from the dead goes to them, they will repent." But he told him, "If they don't listen to Moses and the prophets, they will not be persuaded if someone rises from the dead" (Luke 16:27-31).

At one particular showdown with the Pharisees, we see Jesus' own exasperation with those who said that if He would just give them proof, they would believe:

The Pharisees came out and began to argue with Him, demanding of Him a sign from heaven to test Him. But sighing deeply in His spirit, He said, "Why does this generation demand a sign? I assure you: No sign will be given to this generation!" (Mark 8:11-12)

This absolutely does not mean that we should not want to see signs and wonders. What it does mean is that if we *require* a sign in order to believe, we probably won't get one. And again, *"Jesus said, 'Because you have seen Me, you have believed. Those who believe without seeing are blessed'"* (John 20:29).

In John 3:17-18, Jesus explains that even though He was not sent into the world to judge the world, that when He shows up, the world is judged already. This means that when Jesus steps onto the scene, people whose hearts are already soft toward God will recognize and follow Him, but those whose hearts have already rejected God and His Kingdom will automatically reject Jesus because He is God and represents Him. That's one of the reasons the Pharisees were in such opposition to Him and His ministry.

But is this problem only with people who are staunch unbelievers? Apparently not. In the Book of Second Kings, we have the story of Elisha witnessing up close and personal the miracle of Elijah being taken up to Heaven in a chariot of fire while the "*sons of the prophets*" (the seminary students of the day) watched "*from a distance*" (2 Kings 2:7). Watch what happens next:

> *When the sons of the prophets from Jericho, who were facing him, saw him, they said, "The spirit of Elijah rests on Elisha." They came to meet him and bowed down to the ground in front of him. Then the sons of the prophets said to Elisha, "Since there are 50 strong men here with your servants, please let them go and search for your master. Maybe the Spirit of the LORD has carried him away and put him on one of the mountains or into one of the valleys." He answered, "Don't send [them]." However, they urged him to the point of embarrassment, so he said, "Send [them]." They sent 50 men, who looked for three days but did not find him. When they returned to him in Jericho where he was staying, he said to them, "Didn't I tell you not to go?"* (2 Kings 2:15-18)

Did you get that? The ones who were at a distance refused to believe the one who was right there when it happened!

Amazing! But that's not all. We see the same thing happen in the New Testament, after the Resurrection, when Jesus appears to the disciples:

> *Later, He appeared to the Eleven themselves as they were reclining at the table. He rebuked their unbelief and hardness of heart, because they did not believe those who saw Him after He had been resurrected* (Mark 16:14).

And so it requires a softness of our own hearts just to believe the testimony of those who have seen the activity of God. God forbid that He find a reason to rebuke us while in an atmosphere of His Kingdom.

But what about the people in John 12 who thought it was an angel? Where are they today? Earlier, I mentioned a comment thread on the Internet where someone put out the challenge of growing an amputee's limbs. Further down in that same thread, someone else said something like, "Oh no, I believe this woman walked, because we can do anything we want to when we set our mind to it and believe in ourselves!" Really? Even the reconnection of severed nerves in the spinal cord, as in the case of Delia Knox?

Those are the "must have been an angel" people. They know that something is happening that they can't explain with their own rationality and experience, but they still refuse to identify it as the One True and Living God among us, known and revealed through the life, death, and resurrection of His Son, Jesus Christ. This is what I refer to as the Oprah Winfrey School of Theology. "I am spiritual enough to believe in a spiritual realm, but I refuse to tie it in exclusively to Jesus as the only way to know God."

So then, for those who have seen and heard, and have been witnesses to the love and goodness of God in miraculous ways, what is our response? First, we know that it is not profitable or loving to be angry, defensive, and argumentative with those who do not believe. It is supremely frustrating to have unequivocal, and often medically documented, proof of a miracle and have someone flatly deny it—and you know that nothing you say will change his mind. The classic Phillip Yancey quote is ever true, that "No one ever converted to Christianity because they lost the argument."

So if we can't argue them into truth, what can we do? Well, the Bible says that it is an eye problem. Even Jesus, in John 3 when He explains what it means to be born again, does so in the context of spiritual sight, *"I tell you the truth, no one can see the kingdom of God unless he is born again"* (John 3:3 NIV). As we have already seen, people have already been blinded by the god of this age, and so the remedy is sight, and only the Holy Spirit can give it. And so we pray for them. We pray, not for their comeuppance, not for their humiliation—we pray for them to *see*. We pray that God opens their eyes to see and their ears to hear what He has prepared for them.

However, as it is written: "No eye has seen, no ear has heard, no mind has conceived what God has prepared for those who love Him"—but God has revealed it to us by

His Spirit. The Spirit searches all things, even the deep things of God (1 Corinthians 2:9-10 NIV).

And so, whether we are praying for someone who does not know Jesus yet, or people who are Christian but having difficulty accepting what they see and hear, we can join with apostle Paul in praying one of the most beautiful and powerful prayers ever recorded:

I keep asking that the God of our Lord Jesus Christ, the glorious Father, may give you the Spirit of wisdom and revelation, so that you may know Him better. I pray also that the eyes of your heart may be enlightened in order that you may know the hope to which He has called you, the riches of His glorious inheritance in the saints, and His incomparably great power for us who believe. That power is like the working of His mighty strength (Ephesians 1:17-19 NIV).

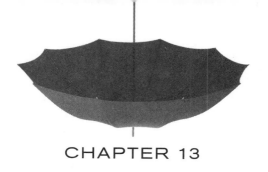

CHAPTER 13

"BUT WE DO SEE JESUS"

Everything we have talked about so far in this book—from the event of revival to the life of revival that is the reality of the Kingdom of God, to the stories of miracles and the hope that the rule of God changes things—all begs the question: What about when it doesn't work? It is a good and valid question, and for the sake of good pastoring, should not be ignored.

One thing we often lack in our quest to believe God for more, and to see more miracles, is a sound, balanced theology of suffering. We need a theology of suffering that does not take away from our wholehearted desire to move in the greatest faith we have ever known and see God move like never before. Thankfully, these two ideals do not cancel each other out. If we are going to truly live in a continual awareness of the presence of the Kingdom of God among us, we can't shy away from the hard questions. To that end, this chapter offers at least one perspective that may release some of the tension between the poles. To do that, let's go to the letter written to the Hebrews.

It helps us to understand first the point of the New Testament book of the letter to the Hebrews. We can't say for sure who wrote it, and though it sounds like Paul and echoes him accurately in places, it doesn't quite fit the literary form of the other writings of Paul. Some say it may have been written by Barnabus. Regardless, the truth and purpose of it remain. This letter was written to Jewish Christians (Hebrews) residing in Rome at about A.D. 66. This would have been the time between the burning of Rome and the siege of Jerusalem. Many scholars agree that Emperor Nero set fire to Rome and blamed it on the Christians to justify their persecution; and in the aftermath, many Christians were horribly martyred, some being set alight while still alive and used as human torches to light Nero's gardens.

In A.D. 70, Rome laid siege to Jerusalem and eventually sacked it, destroying the temple and fulfilling Jesus' prophecy from Matthew 24:1-2:

> *As Jesus left and was going out of the temple complex, His disciples came up and called His attention to the temple buildings. Then He replied to them, "Don't you see all these things? I assure you: Not one stone will be left here on another that will not be thrown down!"*

At that point, when the temple was destroyed, the rituals and sacrifices of the Old Covenant came to an abrupt and screeching halt. No temple, no sacrifice.

The letter to the Hebrews, though, is before the destruction of the temple but during the intense persecution of Christians in Rome. So the Jews who were still holding on to the Old Covenant instead of placing their trust in Christ were trying to persuade the Jewish Christians in Rome to abandon this new "cult" of Christianity and return to Old Covenant Judaism and escape persecution.

The writer of this letter, then, begins an impassioned plea for them not to turn away from the truth that they now know, namely that Jesus is the Messiah, just as they have believed Him to be. Over the course of the letter, the writer will lay out an argument almost like a legal brief, systematically detailing the ways in which Jesus, the Representative of the New Covenant, is superior to what they knew of God in the Old Covenant. His argument is, again, an echo of apostle Paul's statement in Colossians 2:16-17:

> *Therefore don't let anyone judge you in regard to food and drink or in the matter of a festival or a new moon or a sabbath day. These are a shadow of what was to come; the substance is the Messiah.*

The writer to the Hebrews is pleading with these Jewish believers in Rome not to go back to the shadows (the Old Covenant rituals) because there is nothing there to go back to. Jesus had brought a new and better way, and it would be better to die for Him than to live for something that God has said is over.

"DAY AFTER DAY
I'M MORE CONFUSED"

In 1973, singer and songwriter Dobie Gray's answer to his confusion was for the boys to give him a beat to free his soul so that he could drift away. In Hebrews 2:1, the writer makes it clear to the Hebrews that the answer to their confusion was to be careful *not* to drift away, *"We must **therefore** pay even more attention to what we have heard, so that we will not drift away."* What they have already heard is what God has spoken to them in *"these last days"* by His Son (Heb. 1:2). And what has He spoken? That Jesus is the Messiah, superior in every way to what they have known up to now. He goes on to say that:

> *It was first spoken by the Lord and was confirmed to us by those who heard Him. At the same time, God also testi-fied by signs and wonders, various miracles, and distribu-tions [of gifts] from the Holy Spirit according to His will* (Hebrews 2:3b-4).

Now don't miss this. Here comes a very important point of turning, a transitioning statement that we have to see if we are to have any hope of seeing the Kingdom of God invade our reality. In the very next verse (Heb. 2:5), the writer points out something very significant, *"For He has not subjected to angels the world to come that we are talking about."*

And just why is that so significant, you may ask? It is because right there, he equates the signs, wonders, miracles, and gifts of the Holy Spirit with the manifestation now of the *"world to come."* Do you see it? He is talking about God displaying the reality of His Kingdom *now* to testify of the Messiahship and ultimate superiority of His only begotten Son! But even that isn't the most explosive part of this passage.

Get ready. Here it comes. And please don't do what I sometimes do and skip over this next Scripture quote just because you have already read Hebrews and you think you know it. Look at it slowly, carefully:

> *For He has not subjected to angels the world to come that we are talking about. But one has somewhere testified.[23] What is man, that You remember him, or the son of man, that You care for him? You made him lower than the angels for a short time; You crowned him with glory and honor and subjected everything under his feet. For in subjecting everything to him, He left nothing not subject to him. As it is, we do not yet see everything subjected to him. But we do see Jesus—made lower than the angels for a short time so that by God's grace He might taste death for everyone—crowned with glory and honor because of the suffering of death* (Hebrews 2:5-9).

CAUTION: CAREFUL INTERPRETATION REQUIRED

If we are not careful, we will read this passage too quickly and assume that the reference here regarding who is crowned and to whom everything is subject is about Jesus. It isn't. But don't panic! I absolutely hold in high regard the lordship of

Jesus, which you will already know from this book unless you just picked it up and are reading this chapter first.

Here's the key: In this particular quote, *"son of man"* refers to man, not Jesus as the Son of Man. Want to see it for yourself? Find a good translation of the Bible, such as Holman Christian Standard Bible and the New King James Version, that capitalizes proper nouns referring to the Godhead (Father, Son, Holy Spirit). You will see (as in the quote above) that the "him" of this passage is lowercase. It does not refer to Jesus. Once we see that, the rest of the passage makes sense. So, with that distinction, allow me to rephrase verses 6-8:

> What is mankind, that You remember him, or the son of mankind, that You care for him? You made (us) lower than the angels for a short time; You crowned (us) with glory and honor and subjected everything under (our) feet. (Here the writer ends his quote and goes on to say) For in subjecting everything to (us), He left nothing not subject to (us).

If you don't believe me about that interpretation, do a little bit of research and word study on it for yourself. Go ahead. I'll wait.

OK, we're back. So the big, audacious point of this passage is that God, by His own authority and by the blood of His Son, has given back to us the authority over creation that Adam gave away and that Jesus bought back for us on the cross. Jesus had no need to buy back His own authority because He never lost it. He bought back ours and delivered it to us as reigning children of the Father.

But therein lies the problem. You see, the Scripture says that in subjecting everything to us, He (God) left *nothing not subject to us!* Two negatives equals a positive. In other words, everything is subject to us. There is absolutely *nothing* that is *not* subject to us in our authority as ambassadors of another Kingdom, as kings and priests in this world, as the temple of God in the earth, the place where people meet Him through our lives and the word of our testimonies. So what does "everything" include? Well...everything! Sin, disease, injustice, depression, hopelessness, addictions, deception, and the list goes on. Reminds me of Luke 10:19: *"Look, I have given you the authority to trample on snakes and scorpions and over all the power of the enemy; nothing will ever harm you."* Which is a great transition to the big point of this chapter.

Look at the last part of Luke 10:19 again, *"Nothing will ever harm you."* Do you know to whom He was speaking? Well, among others, His closest 12 disciples. So what happened to them? All but one, John, died horrible deaths as willing and joyful martyrs for their Lord, not counting Judas Iscariot. Was Jesus lying then? Was He just playing them so that they would hang around? Of course not. Literally, what it means is, "I am giving you authority over every plan of the enemy, and you will all be able to fulfill the assignments that you will get from Me to take the Gospel into all the world. Be sure of this one thing: The enemy will not be able to defeat you!"

AND YET...

And yet, it seems that sometimes, even when we believe all the right things, confess all the right things, pray the right phrases, and move in the authority we know is ours, a loved one dies. The job is lost. A husband continues to make the wrong choices. The young mother next door sinks deeper into depression. Cancer doesn't go away.

How can we believe that everything is subject to us when it doesn't seem to bow?

If you have ever felt that pang of despair, that sting of confusion, that conflict between what you know to be true of the Kingdom of God and the reality of your present experience, then read on in Hebrews 2. Let the next part of verse 8 and the first part of verse 9 wash over you like a cool breeze on an August afternoon, as you hear the same confession from the great writer of this letter to the Hebrews: *"As it is, we do not yet see everything subjected to him* [us]. *But we do see Jesus..."*

And there it is. The simplicity of the sovereignty of God and the majesty of Jesus, being applied like a soothing balm to the burn of our disappointment. *"We do not yet see everything subjected to* [us]. *But we do see Jesus."* Even this author of biblical text acknowledges the present level of experience that must be all too real for the persecuted Jewish believers in Rome. "If everything is subject to us, then why is Nero still on the throne of Rome? Why are our friends still disappearing in the middle of the night? Why are our husbands and wives and children being struck down by lions and swords?"

The beauty of this passage is that the writer does not try to answer each objection, each question, because he has no answers to give. Again, we hear the echo of Paul in Second Corinthians 4:8: *"We are pressured in every way but not crushed; we are perplexed but not in despair."* When Paul says they are perplexed, that means they are "without answer." And in that place of looking for answers, there is only one good place to set our eyes—"But we do see Jesus."

And now the phrase about being made lower than the angels *does* refer to Jesus, in order to emphasize that He became one of us in His incarnation so that He might *"taste death for everyone"* (again, us). So the question we must ask ourselves is, what does Jesus reign over? What exactly is subject to Him? The answer, of course, is just like before—everything! Except the difference is that Jesus, in His very real experience, lives and reigns over every darkened corner, over every hopeless hospital room, over every solemn, rose-scented funeral parlor. He reigns.

In reality, in actuality, experientially, without exception, nothing whatsoever threatens His rule or can pretend to try to usurp His authority. Nothing—no cancer, no job loss, no depression, no blindness, no paralysis, no addiction, no diagnosis—nothing in this world can assail His rule. And so, when we cannot see victory in our own experience, we see it in His. And we know that we are, by the rights of grace, there with Him in all of His victories.

God forbid that we ever lower the truth of the superiority of Christ to the level of our own experience. We may not yet see everything subject to us, but what we see is not all there is. And so we must see more. We must see Jesus, ruling and reigning over the things that it seems have ruled over us. And in that seeing, we regain our hope. For we know that He rules a Kingdom in which we are more than just citizens. We are co-rulers, joint heirs. We are brothers and sisters of the Son of God. *"For the One who sanctifies and those who are sanctified all have one Father. That is why He is not ashamed to call them brothers"* (Heb. 2:11).

And so, when we see correctly, when we get our eyes off our disappointment and put them squarely on the One who never disappoints and who has already defeated our enemy, we believe again. We pray again. We declare again. We stand again. We fight again. And we do not *"get tired of doing good, for we will reap at the proper time if we don't give up"* (Gal. 6:9).

As Bill Johnson has said, we take our disappointment back into the throne room of God, and we ask Him to do whatever it takes in us for us to be able to walk in more and more experience of the victory and reality of the Kingdom of God so that, one day, when we come up against that thing that looks like it won, that on that day, we stand against it again. And because it is defeated in Jesus' experience, and we reign with Him—when Heaven invades earth again—on that day, we get to see it fall in our experience, too. Cancer disappears. Depression flies away. Addictions shatter. Joy returns. Husbands come home. Blind eyes open. Children give their hearts to Jesus. And the things that once seemed so daunting, bow their knees to the lordship of the only begotten Son of the One True and Living God.

> *O soul, are you weary and troubled?*
> *No light in the darkness you see?*
> *There's light for a look at the Savior,*
> *And life more abundant and free!*
>
> *Turn your eyes upon Jesus,*
> *Look full in His wonderful face,*
> *And the things of earth will grow strangely dim,*
> *In the light of His glory and grace.*
>
> *Through death into life everlasting*
> *He passed, and we follow Him there;*
> *O'er us sin no more hath dominion—*
> *For more than conqu'rors we are!*
>
> *Turn your eyes upon Jesus,*
> *Look full in His wonderful face,*
> *And the things of earth will grow strangely dim,*
> *In the light of His glory and grace.*
>
> *His Word shall not fail you—He promised;*
> *Believe Him, and all will be well:*
> *Then go to a world that is dying,*
> *His perfect salvation to tell!*

THE NEW NORMAL

Turn your eyes upon Jesus,
Look full in His wonderful face,
And the things of earth will grow strangely dim,
In the light of His glory and grace.

—Helen H. Lemmel, 1922

CHAPTER 14

PAST IS PROLOGUE

"Whereof what's past is prologue; what to come,
In yours and my discharge."

—William Shakespeare
The Tempest Act 2, scene 1, 245–254

In Romans chapter 14, apostle Paul is encouraging the Christians in Rome to live by their consciences before God, and not to worry about how other people are evaluating their righteousness against their own standards. Thus he tells them, *"Therefore, do not let your good be slandered, for the kingdom of God is not eating and drinking, but **righteousness, peace, and joy** in the Holy Spirit"* (Rom. 14:16-17). This is just one instance of Scripture helping us understand the nature of the rule and reign of God in our lives. Many more examples abound, including the parables Jesus told, stories that illustrate in powerful ways the nature of the Kingdom.

It is this passage in Romans in particular, though, that I want to focus on here. As I look at the revivals of history, it seems evident that if we look at them through Kingdom lenses, we will see that each one of them manifested a certain aspect of the Kingdom of God. That manifestation was intended by God to be a new level of living from which we would all proceed to the next. Three revivals, or moves of God, illustrate the nature of the Kingdom as presented in Romans 14:16-17—righteousness, peace, and joy.

RIGHTEOUSNESS

From 1904-1906, the Welsh Revival spread through the south of Great Britain like a redeeming wildfire. Primarily through the ministry of three young men, Dan Roberts, Sydney Evans, and Evan Roberts, thousands would be swept into churches and into citizenship in the Kingdom of God. In his book *The World Aflame,* Rick Joyner tells us that "James Stewart, a historian of the Welsh Revival, researched the newspapers and magazines published in Wales in 1904 and 1905 and could not find a single advertisement promoting meetings."[24] The leaders of the revival depended solely upon God Himself for their direction on how to proceed at every juncture. In fact, "they sought the Lord daily for His will and they went where He told them to go. They knew that apart from the presence and power of the Holy Spirit they would accomplish nothing.

When they arrived in a place, sometimes they preached and sometimes they did not. Sometimes they kept silent during the entire services which often lasted four or five hours."[25]

Over the course of the revival, whole cities were dramatically impacted. Bars and theaters closed for lack of business, crime rates plummeted, police were rarely needed, drunkards became sober, and gamblers stopped gambling. Conviction of sin and deep repentance were the order of the day, and the evidence supports the conclusion that the Welsh Revival was a work of God that embodied a specific aspect of the Kingdom—righteousness.

The Welsh Revival is by no means the only revival in history marked by conviction, holiness, and righteousness, nor was it the only mark of that revival. Others include the Great Awakening of 1858, where it was said that Charles Finney could walk into a factory and the production would come to a halt as the workers would fall to their knees and inquire how to be saved. In more recent history is the Brownsville Revival, or the Father's Day Outpouring at Brownsville Assembly of God in Pensacola, Florida.

When I heard that revival was happening in Pensacola, my heart leapt within me. I purposed immediately to go to it, even though it was happening at a place and with manifestations that were outside of my denominational experience. The overriding factor, though, was the report that thousands of people were running to the altar each night, broken before the Lord, giving their hearts to Jesus.

As a good Southern Baptist boy, born and pedigreed, I knew I could look past all the other goings-on if people were getting saved. John Kilpatrick, the pastor of Brownsville Assembly at the time, writes in his book, *Feast of Fire*, about Evangelist Steve Hill, the man who preached the Brownsville Revival:

> Every night, one thing is certain, Steve opens the altar, first, for any sinner who wants to receive the gift of salvation and conversion. I have never seen a man with as much passion for lost souls as Steve. He loves sinners with incredible depths, maybe because of his own sense of depravity before he came to Jesus. To listen to Steve feels like you are listening to a Finney or a Moody or a Whitefield because he has such a fervor for the lost. I have never seen a more effective altar call in my life.[26]

The Kingdom character of righteousness was a clarion call every night for the five years of the Brownsville Revival.

PEACE

In 2002, after pastoring in the North Dallas, Texas, area for about ten years, my wife and I sensed a call from the Lord to move back to our hometown of Mobile, Alabama, and plant a church. As we talked about a possible name for the church, I began to recount some of the watershed moments in my walk with the Lord, moments that had defined me. One of those occurred as I sat in a beanbag chair in my apartment as a freshman in college, being transformed as I read *The Master's*

Indwelling by Andrew Murray. Murray was another part of my introduction to what I had heard referred to as the Deeper Life Movement. Thus, the name of our new church plant became Deeper Life Fellowship.

Through the 1970s, I had the privilege of sitting under the teaching of a great number of spiritual giants who helped walk me down the road of victorious Christian living: Vance Havner, Bertha Smith, Roy Hession, Major Ian Thomas, Peter Lord, Leonard Ravenhill, Jack Taylor, Jim Hylton, and Dudley Hall among them. I became aware of the idea that we can indeed live a revived life every day; and as I studied, I found that it was not a new idea, but one that had its roots in a movement called the Keswick Convention.

In the early 1870s, the British Isles had felt the impact of ministries like those of D.L. Moody and Ira Sankey, as well as being influenced by what was being called the "Higher Life." Instrumental in this was a book written by W.E. Boardman, *The Higher Christian Life.* As a result, in 1867, Robert Pearsall Smith and his wife became convinced of the Lord that the daily fight against sin is not won by struggling, but by faith. It was the same faith, they came to see, that appropriated their salvation that also served to break the power of sin in their lives. The same life of Christ that regenerated them was the same life of Christ that was now available to be lived in and through them consistently. Of those who began to be impacted by their message of the Higher Life was Reverend Evan H. Hopkins, who would become one of the leaders in the Keswick Convention.

In 1874, a series of meetings began at which people poured in to hear this message of victory and awakening. One such meeting was held at Oxford, attended by Reverend Canon T.D. Harford-Battersly, Vicar of Saint John's Anglican Church in Keswick, a small town in northern England. Lewis Drummond recounts such in his book *The Awakening That Must Come:*

> He [Harford-Battersly] was radically renewed by the Oxford experience. Here is his own testimony:
>
> "I got a revelation of Christ to my soul, so extraordinary, so glorious, and precious, that from that day it illuminated my life. I found He was all I wanted; I shall never forget it; the day and hour are present with me. How it humbled me and yet what peace it brought." The Keswick Convention was about to be born.[27]

Some of the monumental figures of the faith came out of this movement: F.B. Meyer, Andrew Murray, G. Campbell Morgan, R.A. Torrey, and contemporaries like John Stott and Stephen Olford.[28] However, and here is where it dovetails with our purpose in this work, the revival that was the Higher Life movement was, essentially, a prolonged spike in the activity of God in reviving, and seemed not to grow into a full Kingdom expression of the rest of the Body of Christ rising to live at that level and go on from there.

In this vein, Drummond writes:

> One thing deeply disturbs me about the Keswick movement however. I have been forced to conclude, along

with the renewal and charismatic movements, Keswick has touched only the hungry few. Despite its strength and worldwide influence, Keswick has not moved the mainstream of the church. The average congregation still flows along in its river of mediocrity and lethargy. Keswick simply has not transformed and revived the entire church of God. Where, oh where, is the revival we need? Will the awakening that must come ever dawn?[29]

I believe that it is dawning, but it is necessarily taking on a different form from before. Instead of a series of meetings, revival, as a revelation of the continual presence and Kingdom of God, is increasing. And part of the increase is an aspect of the Kingdom by which the Keswick Convention and the Higher Life and Deeper Life movements were marked—the peace of God.

JOY

About a year and a half before the revival in Pensacola, another outpouring had begun in January 1994—the Toronto Blessing, or what came to be known as the Father's Blessing. It quickly became a point of controversy that one of the central manifestations at the Toronto Airport Vineyard, pastored by John and Carol Arnott, was "holy laughter." This phenomenon had been seen most recently in the meetings of Rodney Howard-Browne, and had subsequently become part of the move at Toronto.

While the laughter was frowned upon by more traditional streams, it became evident right away that God Himself was doing a work of refreshing in the people who attended.

Respondents to a 1995 survey conducted on nearly 1,000 visitors to the Toronto church confirmed this impression. Approximately half of those who filled out the questionnaires indicated that they had come to Toronto feeling "spiritual dryness and great discouragement," but most left reporting great refreshing. Nearly nine out of ten respondents indicated that they were "more in love with Jesus now than I have ever been in my life," that they had "come to know the Father's love in new ways."[30]

In Acts 3:19, Peter preaches about this very thing: "*Therefore repent and turn back, that your sins may be wiped out so that seasons of refreshing may come from the presence of the Lord.*" Further, the psalmist cries out to God, "*Will You not revive us again so that Your people may rejoice in You?*" (Ps. 85:6). Often in past moves of God, the Lord has demonstrated to us the Kingdom quality of joy and invited us up into it—if we will recognize it and follow.

HOBBITS AND THE NEW NORMAL

Recently, my wife and I watched again *The Return of the King*, the last film in Peter Jackson's epic portrayal of J.R.R. Tolkien's *Lord of the Rings* trilogy, and I was struck by a scene that occurs at the very end of the film. The hobbits have just finished a journey and a quest unlike any hobbits that have ever come before them. They have befriended elves, dwarves, and kings of men. They have fought and defeated the greatest evil, slain monstrous Orcs, and survived the hardships of Mount Doom. And finally, after heaving the Ring of Power into the fires of Mordor, forever destroying its power to corrupt, they have made their way back home to their beloved shire, a quaint community of peaceful little people who live quaint, peaceful little lives, completely unaware of the mysteries and adventures beyond the borders of their town. And yet, as these four hobbits sit in the pub that they have known so well their whole lives, in the company of townspeople whom they have known so well their whole lives, they look around, and you can see on their faces, that for them, things are not the same as they were before they left. Yes, the village is the same, the people are the same, but they, themselves, are different. They have been changed forever by their adventure, they have seen far more than what had satisfied them before, and they cannot un-see what they have seen. Their experience, their very worldview, has been forever altered because they have lived a bigger life than the shire could ever contain again.

And so it is with the Kingdom of God. When we leave our comfortable little theologies, our quaint and peaceful compartments of lower level living, we enter a quest that takes us to places in the Lord and in His rule and reign that we had never dreamed we would ever see. Parkinson's disappears. Paralytics walk. Families are restored. Addictions are broken in an instant.

We stand amazed, speechless, at the bigness of our God. And once we have seen, even for a moment, Heaven invade earth, we cannot go back to our quaint, figured-out, just-going-to-church-is-enough-for-me lives. We have been *"eyewitnesses of His majesty"* (2 Peter 1:16).

CONCLUSION

I am continually encouraged and challenged by the humility and teachable spirit of great men of God who have cast off religious ideas of success and respectability and forsaken all in pursuit of the fullness of Jesus and His Kingdom. One such man is my friend Jim Hylton. It has been said of Jim Hylton that, at one time, he had seen more "revival" or "spiritual awakening" than any man alive in America.[31] I find it fitting to nod to one of my fathers in the faith and allow Jim to reiterate my thoughts on revival and the Kingdom of God for you here:

> The wide world of Kingdom awareness awaits us as we awaken. Trying to compress the Kingdom of God into Church life as we now know it would be like trying to compress a sprawling, 50-square-mile city into a one-half-square-mile village. Our vision is too small and our agenda is too limited. We are to awaken to something bigger than revival and self-consciousness. Our awakening to Christ and the Kingdom, His life in action, is God's goal.[32]

I love revival, because revival is simply the outward expression of the invisible Kingdom of God coming to bear on our reality and changing us in every way. It is not, as we have seen, a series of meetings, nor is it a certain feeling, demonstration, or designation by man. Revival, as Charles Finney has said, is a new beginning of obedience. And revival can continue, undiminished, unabated, as long as we have a Kingdom view, and we allow what we have always called "revival" to flourish, grow, and even morph into something other than what we have traditionally recognized as revival.

In short, revival never has to end, in our hearts and in our world, because revival is the coming of God's rule and reign—His Kingdom—among us. And as the Scriptures so powerfully proclaim:

> *For a child will be born for us, a son will be given to us, and the government will be on His shoulders. He will be named Wonderful Counselor, Mighty God, Eternal Father, Prince of Peace. The dominion will be vast, and its prosperity will never end. He will reign on the throne of David and over his kingdom, to establish and sustain it with justice and righteousness from now on and forever. The zeal of the LORD of Hosts will accomplish this* (Isaiah 9:6-7).

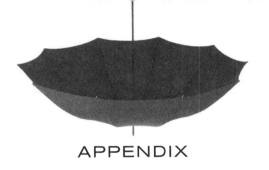

APPENDIX

WHAT THE KINGDOM
IS *NOT*

Even a cursory glance at the available resources about the
Kingdom of God will show that the majority of voices
sounding off are in opposition to it. It is usually lumped in
with historical streams like Dominionism, Christian Reconstructionism, Kingdom Now, Latter Rain, and Joel's Army,
to name a few. So what is it that makes the concept of the
Kingdom presented here different? Is it the same as the movements mentioned above, or are there distinctions? In brief,
there are some notable departures from previous incarnations
of Kingdom theology. We will look here at just one, Christian
Reconstructionism.

Christian Reconstructionism is most closely associated
with Rousas John (R.J.) Rushdoony (1916–2001), and his work

Institutes of Biblical Law (1973). Christian Reconstructionism has been defined "in terms of five theological tenets: a Calvinistic notion of regeneration, or salvation by God-given grace; a postmillennial eschatology predicting that Jesus Christ's second coming will occur after a thousand-year reign of the saints, thus requiring Christians to act now to bring about that reign; presuppositional apologetics; an anti-statist worldview requiring 'decentralized social order where civil government is only one legitimate government among many'; and finally, 'continuing validity and applicability of the whole law of God.'[33]

How does our current revelation of the Kingdom of God compare to these tenets? First, we affirm salvation by grace alone. Second, we hold to the basics of presuppositionalism, which goes back to the apologetics of Cornelius Van Til (1895–1987), namely that a Christian's worldview must necessarily proceed from the starting point of the recognition of God's existence, His sovereignty, and the truth and validity of the Scriptures as they present Him and His reality. Therefore, especially in the realm of apologetics, it is impossible for a Christian to completely separate himself from that mindset in order to find common intellectual ground with the unbeliever. Consequently, the believer, from the basis of those presuppositions, will interpret world systems and events accordingly.

However, Van Tillian presuppositionalism has been used by Christian Reconstructionism to advocate an imposition of Mosaic Law onto all of society, including world governments. This leads to an ideology referred to as anti-statism, where countries worldwide would be ruled by a theonomy, a government based on adherence to biblical (read Old Testament) law.

This obviously presents many problems, not the least of which is strict legalism and the absence of the grace and love that marks the New Testament representation of the Kingdom.

In other words, in the Kingdom of God, love rules, not Old Testament law. Grace and truth walk hand in hand, and it need not be established by the political power brokers to be at work in the world.

Christian Reconstructionism has been named as a contributing factor to the Christian Right movement that was popularized in the 1990s in the United States. This, simply put, was (and still is) a movement that seeks to have laws that allow for immoral practices (such as abortion and the school prayer ban) repealed and replaced with laws that support and endorse a Christian worldview.

Although I am in favor of that happening and would rejoice if it were today, that is not what brings in the Kingdom. The rule and reign of God begins in the hearts of people, not by merely changing the laws that are on the books. In other words, the rule and reign (Kingdom) of God is not imposed onto people externally, but is born in them as they submit to the King and are transformed by having yielded to Him in every area of life.

Subsequently, as people live life, work at their jobs, relate to people, and participate in government out of the flow of the life of God that comes from Him having His way in every part of our hearts, then those people will naturally and supernaturally become influencers in their spheres of influence. This is what contributes to the hopeful eschatology of a Kingdom view. It is not that darkness is winning and we just have to keep our heads down while the world goes to hell and wait for Jesus to come snatch us out of here. He is not coming back to do the work that He told *us* to do:

> *Then Jesus came near and said to them, "All authority has been given to Me in heaven and on earth. Go, therefore, and make disciples of all nations, baptizing them in the name of the Father and of the Son and of the Holy Spirit, teaching them to observe everything I have commanded you. And remember, I am with you always, to the end of the age"* (Matthew 28:18-20).

When the Kingdom of God changes our lives, we become change agents for the Kingdom. People who work in every industry and career field have opportunities—through the victorious life they live submitted to the love of God—to influence the lives and worldviews of people around them and to infuse their work with the truth that has changed them. No coercion, no external requirements to obey Mosaic law, just influence through love and the heart of a servant. This can be said about those in all realms, or kingdoms, of society: government, family, church, education, the marketplace (business), media and technology, sports, financial, and all areas of human endeavor.

All can be impacted from the inside out by the changed lives of Kingdom citizens who see that they are now ambassadors of a greater Kingdom and will, through love and humility, speak and act as representatives of God and His rule and reign.

ENDNOTES

1. Leonard Ravenhill, *Why Revival Tarries* (Minneapolis, MN: Bethany House Publishers, 1996), 27.

2. Philip Greenslade, *A Passion for God's Story* (Tyrone, GA: Paternoster Press, 2002), 145-146.

3. Charles G. Finney, *Revival Lectures* (Grand Rapids, MI: Fleming H. Revell Company, 1979), 7.

4. E. Stanley Jones, *The Unshakable Kingdom and the Unchanging Person* (Bellingham, WA: McNett Press, 1995), 49.

5. Francis McGaw, *John Hyde* (Minneapolis, MN: Bethany House Publishers, 1970), 16.

6. http://www.biblestudytools.com/lexicons/hebrew/nas/
    chayah.html; accessed July 19, 2011.

7. http://www.biblestudytools.com/lexicons/hebrew/kjv/
    paniym.html; accessed July 19, 2011.

8. http://www.biblestudytools.com/lexicons/greek/kjv/
    prosopon.html; accessed July 19, 2011.

9. http://www.biblestudytools.com/lexicons/greek/kjv/
    anapsuxis.html; accessed July 19, 2011.

10. http://www.biblestudytools.com/lexicons/greek/nas/
    erchomai.html; accessed July 19, 2011.

11. http://www.biblestudytools.com/cjb/galatians/5-16.html;
    accessed July 19, 2011.

12. http://www.biotechinstitute.org/what-is-biotechnology/
    glossary/y; accessed July 19, 2011.

13. George Dana Boardman, *The Kingdom (Basileia); An
    Exegetical Study* (New York: Charles Scribner's Sons, 1899),
    226.

14. Ibid., 227-228.

15. See Psalm 34:8; 1 Peter 2:3; Hebrews 6:5.

16. George Eldon Ladd, *The Presence of the Future: The
    Eschatology of Biblical Realism* (Grand Rapids, MI: Wm. B.
    Eerdmans Publishing Company, 1959), 110-111.

17. Ibid., 53-54.

18. Bill Johnson, *Dreaming With God* (Shippensburg, PA: Destiny Image Publishers, 2006), 72.

19. Boardman, *The Kingdom,* 227.

20. Ibid., 227-228.

21. For more on this subject, read the excellent works of Dallas Willard, *The Divine Conspiracy*, and J.P. Moreland, *Kingdom Triangle*.

22. To read Lee's firsthand account, visit his website at www.thehealedguy.com.

23. Just a note of encouragement for all of us who have ever forgotten where a Scripture was found but knew it was in there. Here we have a God-inspired author who says something to the effect, "Somewhere in the Bible it says something like this…." Even if you don't always know the address, don't shy away from quoting what you know to be Scripture! (Do quote it accurately and in context, though.)

24. Rick Joyner, *The World Aflame: The Welsh Revival Lessons for Our Times* (Charlotte, NC: Morningstar Publications, 1993), 14.

25. Ibid., 19.

26. John Kilpatrick, *Feast of Fire: The Father's Day Outpouring* (Pensacola, FL: Brownsville Assembly of God, 1995).

27. Lewis A. Drummond, *The Awakening That Must Come* (Nashville, TN: Broadman Press, 1978), 48.

28. Ibid., 49.

29. Ibid., 64.

30. Margaret Poloma, *Toronto Blessing*, Hartford Institute of Religion Research, http://hirr.hartsem.edu/research/pentecostalism_polomaart8.html; accessed July 4, 2011.

31. Jim Hylton, *The Supernatural Skyline: Where Heaven Touches Earth* (Shippensburg, PA: Destiny Image Publishers, Inc., 2010), 31.

32. Ibid., 47.

33. Molly Worthen, "The Chalcedon problem: Rousas John Rushdoony and the origins of Christian reconstructionism," http://www.highbeam.com/doc/1G1-180278685.html; accessed July 4, 2011.

BIBLIOGRAPHY

Biotech Institute. Definition of "yeast." www.biotechinstitute. org/what_is/glossary.html; accessed May 2009.

Boardman, George Dana. *The Kingdom (Basileia); An Exegetical Study*. New York, NY: Charles Scribner's Sons, 1899.

Drummond, Lewis A. *The Awakening That Must Come*. Nashville, TN: Broadman Press, 1978.

Finney, Charles G. *Revival Lectures*. Grand Rapids, MI: Fleming H. Revell Company, 1979.

Greenslade, Philip. *A Passion for God's Story*. Tyrone, GA: Paternoster Press, 2002.

Hylton, Jim. *The Supernatural Skyline: Where Heaven Touches Earth*. Shippensburg, PA: Destiny Image Publishers, Inc., 2010.

Johnson, Bill. *Dreaming With God*. Shippensburg, PA: Destiny Image Publishers, 2006.

Jones, E. Stanley. *The Unshakable Kingdom and the Unchanging Person*. Bellingham, WA: McNett Press, 1995.

Joyner, Rick. *The World Aflame: The Welsh Revival Lessons for Our Times*. Charlotte, NC: Morningstar Publications, 1993.

Kilpatrick, John. *Feast of Fire: The Father's Day Outpouring*. Pensacola, FL: Brownsville Assembly of God, 1995.

Ladd, George Eldon. *The Presence of the Future: The Eschatology of Biblical Realism*. Grand Rapids, MI: Wm. B. Eerdmans Publishing Company, 1959.

McGaw, Francis. *John Hyde*. Minneapolis, MN: Bethany House Publishers, 1970.

Merriam-Webster Online Dictionary, http://www.m-w.com/dictionary/critic (2007).

Poloma, Margaret M. *Toronto Blessing*. Hartford Institute of Religion Research; http://hirr.hartsem.edu/research/pentecostalism_polomaart8.html; accessed July 4, 2011.

Ravenhill, Leonard. *Why Revival Tarries*. Minneapolis, MN: Bethany House Publishers, 1996.

Worthen, Molly. "The Chalcedon problem: Rousas John Rushdoony and the origins of Christian reconstructionism." High Beam Research; http://www.highbeam.com/doc/1G1-180278685.html; accessed July 4, 2011.

ABOUT DR. MARK WYATT

Mark Wyatt is a native of Mobile who was raised under the ministry of Fred Wolfe at Cottage Hill Baptist Church. Mark was called to ministry while at a retreat with Leonard Raven-hill and has always felt that the themes of revival, surrender, and freedom in Christ are integral parts of his spiritual DNA. Mark married Mary Ann Varner in 1986, received his B.A. in Speech Communication from Auburn University, and taught in the singles department of Cottage Hill until his departure for seminary in 1989. Moving to Fort Worth, Texas, Mark received his Master's Degree in Communication from Southwestern Baptist Theological Seminary in December of 1991.

After graduating, he was invited to join the staff of Sagamore Hill Baptist Church in Fort Worth where he served for three years as Minister to Singles and Media Minister, and later Minister of Pastoral Care.

In January 1994, Mark was called as Senior Pastor of Timbercreek Baptist Church in Flower Mound, Texas. Two years later, while attending revival services at Brownsville Assembly of God in Pensacola, Florida, Mark experienced the presence and mercy of God in a way that changed his life and his church forever. Since then, God has taught him constantly how to pastor a life-giving, city-changing, Jesus-exalting church, helping people come into healthy relationships both with the Lord and each other.

Mark has been a guest lecturer at Southwestern Baptist Theological Seminary in the area of Servant Evangelism. Under his pastorate, Timbercreek pioneered a ministry to skaters that saw over 650 teenagers and parents come to faith in Christ in three years. In 2001, Timbercreek Church was named in the top 4% of churches in America in the area of evangelism by the Billy Graham School of Evangelism and Discipleship. The church has been featured in the Dallas media a number of times, including the Dallas Morning News and other papers and magazines. Currently, Pastor Mark is pursuing a Ph.D. in Pastoral Ministry from Atlantic Coast Seminary.

Mark and Mary Ann have four children: Samuel, Sarah, Nathaniel, and Autumn.

Pastor Mark serves on the Advisory Board of several organizations, including the Fellowship of Connected Churches and Ministries, The Opportunity for Unity, and PowerSurge 100.

YOU MAY CONTACT DR. MARK WYATT AT:

Deeper Life Fellowship

3350 Dawes Rd., Mobile, AL 36695

www.deeperlifefellowship.com

251-634-1002

Email: pastormark@deeperlifefellowship.com

IN THE RIGHT HANDS, THIS BOOK WILL CHANGE LIVES!

Most of the people who need this message will not be looking for this book. To change their lives, you need to put a copy of this book in their hands.

> *But others (seeds) fell into good ground, and brought forth fruit, some a hundred-fold, some sixty-fold, some thirty-fold* (Matthew 13:8).

Our ministry is constantly seeking methods to find the good ground, the people who need this anointed message to change their lives. Will you help us reach these people?

> *Remember this—a farmer who plants only a few seeds will get a small crop. But the one who plants generously will get a generous crop* (2 Corinthians 9:6).

EXTEND THIS MINISTRY BY SOWING
3 BOOKS, 5 BOOKS, 10 BOOKS, OR MORE TODAY,
AND BECOME A LIFE CHANGER!

Thank you,

Don Nori Sr., Founder
Destiny Image
Since 1982